आ नो भद्राः क्रतवो यन्तु विश्वतः ।

ā no bhadrāḥ kratavo yantu viśvataḥ

Let noble thoughts come to us from every side

- Ṛg Veda I - 89-i

BHAVAN'S BOOK UNIVERSITY

STORIES OF VIKRAMADITYA

[VETALA PANCHAVIMSATI]

BHAVAN'S BOOK UNIVERSITY

STORIES OF VIKRAMADITYA

[VETALA PANCHAVIMSATI]

2025

BHARATIYA VIDYA BHAVAN
Kulapati Munshi Marg
Mumbai - 400007

Bharatiya Vidya Bhavan
Kulapati Munshi Marg
Mumbai - 400007

First Edition	:	*1963*
Second Edition	:	*1964*
Third Edition	:	*1969*
Fourth Edition	:	*1973*
Fifth Edition	:	*1990*
Sixth Edition	:	*1995*
Seventh Edition	:	*2001*
Eighth Edition	:	*2008*
Ninth Edition	:	*2019*
Tenth Edition	:	*2025*

Price : **₹310/-**

Typesetting by Samir Parekh,
at Creative Page Setters

PRINTED IN INDIA

by Siddhi Printers, 13/14, Bhabha Building, 13th Khetwadi Lane, Mumbai - 400004
and Published by P. V. Sankarankutty, Director, for Bharatiya Vidya Bhavan,
Kulapati K. M. Munshi Marg, Mumbai - 400007.
E-mail: publications@bhavans.info
Website: www.bhavans.info

KULAPATI'S PREFACE

The Bharatiya Vidya Bhavan – that Institute of Indian Culture in Mumbai – needed a Book University, a series of books which, if read, would serve the purpose of providing higher education. Particular emphasis, however, was to be put on such literature as revealed the deeper impulsions of India. As a first step, it was decided to bring out in English 100 books, 50 of which were to be taken in hand almost at once.

It is our intention to publish the books we select, not only in English, but also in the following Indian languages: Hindi, Bengali, Gujarati, Marathi, Tamil, Telugu, Kannada and Malayalam.

This scheme, involving the publication of 900 volumes, requires ample funds and an all-India organization. The Bhavan is exerting its utmost to supply them.

The objectives for which the Bhavan stands are the reintegration of the Indian culture in the light of modern knowledge and to suit our present day needs and the resuscitation of its fundamental values in their pristine vigour.

Let me make our goal more explicit:

We seek the dignity of man, which necessarily

implies the creation of social conditions which would allow him freedom to evolve along the lines of his own temperament and capacities: we seek the harmony of individual efforts and social relations, not in any makeshift way, but within the framework of the Moral Order; we seek the creative art of life, by the alchemy of which human limitations are progressively transmuted, so that man may become the instrument of God, and is able to see Him in all and all in Him.

The world, we feel, is too much with us. Nothing would uplift or inspire us so much as the beauty and aspiration which such books can teach.

In this series, therefore, the literature of India, ancient and modern, will be published in a form easily accessible to all. Books in other literatures of the world, if they illustrate the principles we stand for, will also be included.

This common pool of literature, it is hoped, will enable the reader, eastern or western, to understand and appreciate currents of world thought, as also the movements of the mind in India, which, though they flow through different linguistic channels, have a common urge and aspiration.

Fittingly, the Book University's first venture is the *Mahabharata*, summarised by one of the greatest living Indians, C. Rajagopalachari; the second work is on a section of it, the *Gita*, by H. V. Divatia, an eminent jurist and a student of philosophy. Centuries ago, it was proclaimed of the *Mahabharata:* "What is not in it, is nowhere." After twenty five centuries, we can use the same words about it. He who knows it not, knows not the heights and depths of the soul; he misses the trials and tragedy and the beauty and grandeur of life.

The *Mahabharata* is not a mere epic; it is a romance, telling the tale of heroic men and women and of some who were divine; it is a whole literature in itself, containing a code of life, a philosophy of social and ethical relations, and speculative thought on human problems that is hard to rival; but, above all, it has for its core the *Gita*, which is, as the world is beginning to find out, the noblest of scriptures and the grandest of sagas in which the climax is reached in the wondrous Apocalypse in the Eleventh Canto.

Through such books alone the harmonies underlying true culture, I am convinced, will one day reconcile the disorders of modern life.

I thank all those who have helped to make this new branch of the Bhavan's activity successful.

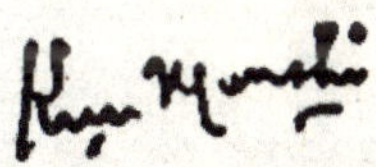

Publisher's Note

These Stories of King Vikramaditya appeared in the *Bhavan's Journal* under the caption of *"Vetala Panchavimsati."*

We have pleasure in issuing the same in our Book University Series in response to the demand of the reading public to have the stories in book form.

INTRODUCTORY TALE

There was a city named Dharanagar, the king of which was Gandharb Sen. He had four queens, and by them six sons, one more learned and more powerful than the other. Fate ruled: after some days the king died, and his eldest son, Shank by name, became king. Again, after some days, a younger brother, Vikram, after slaying his eldest brother, himself became king, and began to govern well. Day by day his dominion so increased that he became king of all India; and, after setting up his government on a firm basis, he inaugurated an epoch.

After some time the king thought that he ought to visit those countries of which he had heard.[1]

Having decided on this, he made over his throne to his younger brother Bharthari, and himself assuming the guise of a devotee, set out to wander from land to land and forest to forest.

A Brahman was practising austerities in that city. One day a deity brought and presented to him the fruit of immortality. He then took the fruit home and said to his wife, "Whoever will eat this will become immortal; the deity told me this at the time of giving the fruit." Hearing this the

1. *Lit* – The king thought, "I should travel over those countries whose names I am hearing."

Brahman's wife wept excessively, and began to say "This is a great evil we have to suffer! For, becoming immortal, how long shall we go on begging alms? Nay, to die is better than this; if we die, then we escape from the trials of the world". Then the Brahman said, "I took the fruit and brought it; but hearing your words, I am bereft of understanding. Now I will do whatever you bid me do." Then his wife said to him, "Give this fruit to the king, and in exchange for it take wealth, whereby we may enjoy the advantages of this world as well as those of the world to come."

Hearing this, the Brahman went to the king and gave him his blessing; and after explaining the virtues of the fruit, he said, "Great king! If you take this fruit and give me some wealth, you will live long and I shall be happy". The king, having given the Brahman a lakh of rupees and dismissed him, entered the female apartments, and giving the fruit to the queen whom he loved most, said "O queen! Do eat this, for thou wilt become immortal, and wilt continue young for ever." The queen, hearing this, took the fruit from the king and he returned to his court.

A certain *kotwal* was the paramour of that queen: to him she gave the fruit. It so happened that a courtesan was the kotwal's mistress; he gave the fruit to her and described its virtues. That courtesan thought to herself that the fruit was a fitting present for the king. Having determined on this, she went to the king, and presented the fruit. His majesty took the fruit and gave her much wealth; and contemplating the fruit, he became sick of the world, and began to say, "The perishable wealth of this world is of no use whatever; for through it one must ultimately fall into the pit of hell. Preferable to this is the practising of religious duties and the binding in the remembrance of the Deity, whereby it may be well in the future".

Coming to this conclusion, he entered the female apartments and asked the queen what she had done with the fruit he gave her. She replied, "I ate it up". Then the king showed the queen that fruit. She, setting her eyes on it, stood aghast, and was unable to make any reply. Then the king had the fruit washed and ate it, and abandoning his kingdom and throne, assumed the guise of a devotee, and betook himself to the jungle, unaccompanied and alone, without communicating his plan to anyone.

The throne of Vikram became vacant. When this news reached king Indra, he sent a demon to guard Dharanagar. He kept watch over the city day and night. To be brief, the report spread from country to country that king Bharthari had abandoned his government and gone away. King Vikrama, too, heard the news, and immediately came to his country. It was then midnight: he was entering the city at that hour, when the demon called out, "Who art thou? and whither goest thou? Stand still, and mention thy name". Then the king said, "It is I, king Vikram; I am entering my own city: who art thou to challenge me." Then the demon replied, "The deities have sent me to guard this city; if you are really king Vikram, first fight with me, and then enter the city."

On hearing these words the king tightened his waistband and challenged the demon. Thereupon the demon, too, stood up to him. The battle began. At last the king threw the demon down and sat upon his breast. Then he said, "O king! thou hast brought me low; I grant thy life as a boon". Upon this the king, laughing, said "Thou are gone mad; whose life does thou grant?" Did I will, I could slay thee; how canst thou grant me life?" Then the demon said, "O king! I am about to save thee from death; first attend to a tale of mine, and thereafter rule over the whole world free from all care." At length the king set him free, and began to listen attentively to his tale.

Then the demon addressed him thus:

"There was in this city a very liberal king, named Chandrabhan. One day he went forth casually into the jungle; When, what should he behold but an ascetic hanging, head downwards, from a tree, and sustaining himself by inhaling smoke alone – neither receiving anything from any one, nor speaking to any one. Perceiving this state of his, the king returned home and seating himself in his court, said, 'whoever will bring this ascetic here shall receive a lakh of rupees.' A courtesan hearing these words, came to the king and spake thus: 'If I obtain your majesty's leave, I will have a child begotten by that ascetic and bring it here mounted on his shoulder'.

"The king was astonished to hear this speech, and binding the courtesan in fulfillment of her contract of bringing the ascetic, dismissed her by giving her a betel-leaf. She went to that wild region, and reaching the ascetic's place perceived that he was really hanging head-downwards, neither eating nor drinking anything, and that he was withered up. In short, that courtesan prepared some sweetmeat and put it into the ascetic's mouth: finding it sweet, he ate it up with zest. Thereupon, the courtesan offered more to his mouth. Thus for two days did she continue feeding him with a sweetmant, by eating which he gained a certain degree of strength. Then, opening his eyes, and descending from the tree, he inquired of her. 'What business has brought thee hither?'

"The courtesan replied, 'I am the daughter of a god; I was practising religious austerities in heaven; I have now come into this wild'. The devotee said again, 'Where is thy hut? Show it to me.' Thereupon, the courtesan brought the ascetic to her hut, and commenced feeding him with savoury viands, so that the ascetic left off inhaling smoke, and took to eating food and drinking water daily. Eventually Cupid troubled him, upon which he had carnal desire, which disturbed his austere practices; and the courtesan became pregnant. In ten months a boy was born, and when he was some months old, the courtesan said to the devotee, 'O saint! You should now set out on a pilgrimage whereby all the sins of the flesh may be blotted out.'

'Deluding him with such words, she mounted the boy on his shoulder and started for the king's court, whence she had set out pledged to accomplish this. When she came before the king, his majesty recognised her from a distance and seeing the child on the shoulder of the devotee, began saying to the courtiers, 'Just see! This is the very same courtesan who went to bring the devotee!' They replied, 'O king! You are quite right; this is the very same; and be pleased to observe that all that she had stated in your majesty's presence ere she set forth, has come to pass.'

"When the ascetic heard these remarks of the king and courtiers, he perceived that the king had adopted these measures to disturb his religious meditations. With these thoughts in his mind, the devotee returned from thence, and getting out of the city, slew the child, repaired to another jungle, and began to perform peanace. And after some time that king died, and the devotee completed his penance.

"The short of the story is that you three men have been born under one asterism, one conjunction, and in one moment. You took birth in a king's house; the second was an oilman's child; the third, the devotee, was born in a potter's house. You still govern here, while the oilman's son *was* the ruler of the infernal regions; but that potter, bringing his religious meditations to perfection, has killed the oilman, turned him into a demon in a burning ground and placed him hanging head-downwards on a siris-tree, and is intent on killing you. If you escape him, you will rule. I have apprised you of all these circumstances; do not be careless with regard to them". Having narrated thus much, the demon departed and the king entered the private apartments in his palace.

When it was morn, the king came forth and

took his seat on the throne, and gave the order for a general session of the court. As many servants as there were, great and small, all came and made their offerings in his presence, and festive music was played. An extraordinary gladness and rejoicing possessed the whole city, such that in every house, dance, music and songs filled the air. Afer this the king began to govern justly.

It is related that one day an ascetic, named Shantshil, appeared at the king's court with a fruit in his hand, and, presenting the fruit to the king, spread a cloth and sat down there. After a short while he went away. On his departure, the king thought that this was probably the person of whom the demon had spoken. Harbouring this suspicion, he did not eat the fruit, and, summoning the steward, he gave it to him, with instructions to keep it carefully. The devotee, however, came constantly in this same manner, and left a fruit every day.

It so happened that one day the king went to inspect his stable, accompanied by some attendants. During that interval the ascetic, too, arrived there, and presented the king with a fruit in the usual manner. He began tossing it in the air, when all of a sudden it fell from his hand on the ground, and a monkey took it up and broke it in pieces. So exquisite a ruby came out of it that the king and his attendants were astonished at the sight of its brilliance. Thereupon the king said to the devotee, "Why hast thou given me this ruby?"

On this he said, "O great king! It is written in the Shastras that one should not go empty-handed to the following places, viz., those of kings, spiritual teachers, astrologers, physicians and daughters, for at such places one obtains benefit for benefit. Sire! Why do you speak of a single ruby? As many fruits as I have given you, every one of them contains a jewel." Hearing these words, the king asked the steward to bring all the fruits he had given to him. On receiving the king's order, the steward immediately brought them; and, having had the fruits broken open, he found a ruby in each. As he saw so many rubies, the king was excessively pleased, and summoning a tester of precious stones, got the rubies tested, saying the while, "Nothing will accompany one from this world; integrity is the great essential in the world; tell me honestly, therefore the exact value of each gem".

Hearing these words, the jeweller said, "O king! You have spoken the truth. He whose integrity is safe, his all is safe : integrity alone accompanies us, and it is that which proves of advantage in both the worlds. Hear, O king! Each gem is perfect as to colour, stone and form. Were I to declare the value of each to be a crore of rupees, even that would not come up to the mark. In sooth, each gem is worth a clime". Hearing this, the king was pleased beyond measure, and conferring a robe of honour on the jeweller, dismissed him; and taking the devotee's hand, he brought and seated him on the throne, and began thus: "My whole realm is not worth even one of these rubies; tell me, then, what is the reason that you, a religious mendicant, have presented me with so many gems?"

The asetic said, "Your majesty! It is not proper to speak publicly of the following things, viz., magic and incantations, drugs employed in medicines, religious duties, family affairs, the eating of impure meat, evil speech which one has heard – all these things are not spoken of in public; I will tell you in private. Attend! It is a rule that whatever is heard by three pairs of ears remains no secret; the words which reach two pairs of ears no man hears; while the contents of one pair of ears are unknown to Brahman himself, not to speak of man." On hearing these words, the king took the devotee apart and said, "O holy man! You have given me so many rubies, and have not once partaken of food even; you have put me to great shame! Let me know what it is you desire." The ascetic said, "Sire! I am about to practise magic arts in a large cremation ground on the bank of the river Godavari, whereby I shall acquire supernatural powers, and so I beg of you to pass one whole night with me; by your presence near me my magic arts will succeed." Then the king said, "Very well, I wiill come : leave word with me about the day". The ascetic said, "Do you come to me armed and unattended, on Tuesday evening of the dark half of the month Bhadon." The king replied, "You may go; I will surely come, and alone."

Having thus exacted a promise from the king and taken leave, he, for his part, went into a temple and made preparations, and taking all necessaries with him, went and fixed himself in a burning ground; while here the king began to ponder over what had happened. In the meantime, the moment for him to depart arrived. Upon this the king then and there girt his sword, tightened the cloth he wore between his legs, and betook himself alone to the devotee by night, and greeted him. The devotee requested him to be seated, whereupon the king sat down and then perceived goblins, evil spirits, and witches, in various frightful shapes, dancing around; while the ascetic, seated in the centre, was striking two skulls together to keep time. The king felt no fear or alarm on beholding this state of things; but said to the devotee, "What command is there for me?" He replied, "O king! Now that you have come, do this: at a distance of two *kos* south of this place is a burning-ground, wherein is a siris–tree, on which a corpse is suspended; bring that corpse to me at once to this place, where I shall be performing my devotions." Having despatched the king thither, he himself settled down in devotional attitude and began muttering prayers.

For one thing, the darkness of the night was in itself terrifying ; more than this, the down-pour of the rain was as unceasing as if it would rain right through the night: whilst the goblins and ghosts, too, were creating such an uproar that even daring heroes would have been agitated at the spectacle. The king, however, went on his way. The snakes, which kept coming and twining themselves about his legs, he disentangled by repeating incantations. At length, when after passing somehow or other over a perilous road, the king reached the burning-ground, he perceived that goblins were constantly seizing men and destroying them; witches continually munching the livers of children; tigers growling, and elephants screaming. In short, when he noticed the tree, he perceived that leaves and branches of it, from the root to the topmost twig, were burning furiously, while from all four sides arose a tumultuous cry of "Kill him! kill him! Seize him! Take care he does not escape!"

The king was not the least horrified on witnessing that state of things; but he said to himself, "It may or may not be so, but I am convinced this is the same devotee about whom the demon spoke to me." And having gone close and observed, he saw a corpse fastened by a string, and hanging head downwards. He was glad to see the corpse, thinking his trouble had been rewarded. Taking his sword and shield, he climbed the tree fearlessly, and struck such a blow with the sword that the rope was severed and the corpse fell down, and instantly began to weep aloud. On hearing his voice the king was pleased, and said to himself, "Well! This man at least is alive". Then, descending, he enquired of him who he was. He burst out laughing as soon as he heard the question. The king was greatly astonished at this. Again the corpse climbed up the tree and suspended himself. The king, too, that instant climbed up, and clutching him under his arm, brought him down, and said, "Vile wretch! tell me who thou art." He made no reply. The king reflected and said to himself, "Perhaps this is the very oilman whom the demon said the devotee had deposited in the place where bodies are burnt". Thus reflecting, he bound him up in his mantle and brought him to the devotee. The man who displayed such courage should be sure to succeed in his undertakings.

Then the ghoul said, "who art thou? And whither art thou taking me?" The king replied, "I am king Vikram, and am taking thee off to a devotee." He rejoined, "I will go on one condition: if thou utterest a word on the way, I will come straight back". The king agreed to his condition and went off with him. Then the sprite said, "O king! Those who are learned, discerning and wise - their days are passed in the delight of song and the shastras, while the days of the unwise and foolish are spent in dissipation and sleaze. Hence, it is best that this long road should be beguiled by profitable converse: do you attend, O king! to the story I relate."

❒ ❒ ❒

CONTENTS

1. PADMAVATI

Pratapamukuta was king of Varanasi. Mukuta-sekhara was his son; and his queen was Mahadevi. One day the prince, accompanied by the minister's son, went to the chase, and advanced far into a jungle in the midst of which he saw a beautiful tank, on the banks of which wild geese, brahmani ducks, male and female, cranes and water-fowl were, one and all, disporting themselves; on all four sides ghats of solid masonry were constructed: within the tank, the lotus was in full bloom: on the sides were planted trees of different kinds, under the dense shade of which the breezes came cool and refreshing, while birds were warbling on the boughs, and in the forest bloomed flowers of varied hues, on which whole swarms of bees were buzzing. They arrived by the margin of that tank, and washed their hands and faces, and reascended.

On that spot was a temple sacred to Mahadeva. Fastening their horses, and entering the temple, they prayed to Mahadeva and came out. While they were so engaged, a beautiful princess, accompanied by a host of attendants, came to another margin of the tank to bathe; and, having finished her ablutions, meditations and prayers, she, with her own maidens, began to walk about in the shade of the trees.

On this side the minister's son was seated, and the king's son was walking about, when, suddenly, his eyes and the eyes of the princess met.

As soon as he got sight of her beauty, the king's son was fascinated, and began saying to himself, "You wretch, Cupid! why do you molest me?"

And when the princess espied the prince, she took in her hand the lotus-flower which she had fixed on her head after her devotions, placed it in her ear, bit it with her teeth, put it under her foot, then took it up and pressed it to her bosom, and, taking her maidens with her, mounted her chariot and departed.

Unable to understand the implications of the strange action of the princess, the prince sank into the depths of despair, and was overwhelmed with grief on account of her absence. Presently, he came to the minister's son, and with a feeling of shame laid before him the actual state of affairs, saying, 'O friend! I have seen a most beautiful damsel; but I know neither her name nor her abode; should I not possess her, I would give up my life: this I am firmly resolved upon in my mind'.

Hearing this, the minister's son caused him to mount, and brought him home.

But the king's son, made restless by pangs of separation, entirely abandoned writing, reading, eating, drinking, sleeping, the business of government- everything. He used to be constantly sketching her portrait and gazing at it and weeping, not speaking himself, nor listening to what others said.

When the minister's son saw this state of his, he said to him, "Whoever treads the path of love doth not survive; or if he survives, he suffers great sorrow. On this account the wise avoid treading this path."

The king's son, on hearing his words, replied, "In truth, I have entered upon this path, be there joy in it or be there pain."

When he heard this admission, the minister's son said, "Great prince! At the time of leaving did she say anything to you, or you to her?"

Upon this he answered, "I said nothing, nor did I hear anything from her."

Then the minister's son said, "It will be very difficult to find her."

And the king's son stated, "If she be secured, my life will be preserved; otherwise, it is lost."

He enquired again, "Did she make no signs even?"

The prince said, "Yes, these are the gestures she made – suddenly seeing me, she took the lotus-flower from her head, let it touch her ear, bit it with her teeth, placed it under her foot, and pressed it to her bosom."

On hearing this, the minister's son said, "I have comprehended her signs, and discovered her name, habitation, and all about her."

Immensely pleased at this, the prince replied, "Explain to me whatever you have discovered."

Thus he began: "Attend, O king! Her having taken the lotus-flower (Padma) from her head and put it in her ear (Karna) is equivalent to her having informed you that she is an inhabitant of the Karnatak; and in biting it with her teeth (Danta), she intimated that she is the daughter of king Danta-vat; and by pressing it under her foot, she declared that her name is Padmavati; and in again taking it up and pressing it to her bosom, she informed you that you dwell in her heart."

The prince was in transports of joy to hear this interpretation. But where was she? Could he be considered happy in his present state? – No, not till he was in her presence. To this effect he said, "I entreat you to take me to the city in which she dwells."

No sooner had he said this than both dressed themselves, girt themselves with arms, and taking some jewels with them, mounted their horses and took the road to Karnatak.

After several days they reached Karnatak. And having arrived below the palaces of the king in their stroll through the city, they met an old woman sitting at her door and plying her cotton-wheel.

The two, dismounting from their horses, approached her and said, "Mother! We are travelling merchants. Our goods are following us; we have come on ahead to seek a lodging; if you will give us a place, we will stay a while."

The old woman looked at their faces and heard their words. This was enough to fill her heart with compassion. She said, "This house is yours; remain here as long as you please."

In short, they entered the house on hearing this; and after some time the old woman came, sat with them; and started chatting with them. On this, the minister's son enquired of her, "What family and relations have you got and how do you subsist?"

The old woman said, " My son is very comfortably provided for in the king's service, and your humble servant is the wet-nurse of Padmavati, the king's daughter. I am pretty old now and therefore remain at home; but the king provides for my maintenance. Once a day, however. I go regularly to see that girl; it is on my return, in my home, alone, that I give vent to my woe."

Hearing these words, the prince rejoiced at heart, and said to the old woman, "When you are starting tomorrow, please carry a message from me too."

She replied, "Son! Why postpone it till tomorrow? I will this moment convey any message of yours that you communicate to me."

Then he said, "Do go and tell her this – the prince whom you saw on the banks of the tank on the fifth day of the bright half of the month Jeth has arrived here."

On hearing these words, the old woman took her stick and went to the palace. When she got there she found the princess sitting alone. Presently, she appeared before her, when the princess saluted her. The old woman gave her her blessing, and said "Daughter! I tended you in your infancy, and suckled you. God has let you grow up; what my heart now desires is that I should see you happy in your prime, then should I, too, receive comfort."

Addressing her in such affectionate words as these, she proceeded to say, "The prince whose heart you took captive on the fifth day of the bright half of Jeth, by the side of the tank, has alighted at my house. He has sent you this message, for you to fulfil the promise you made him, now that he has arrived. And I tell you, for my part, that that prince is worthy of you, and is as excellent in disposition and mental qualities as you are beautiful."

On hearing these words she became angry. Having applied camphor to her hands, she slapped the face of the old woman saying, "Wretch! Get out of my house!"

She rose annoyed, and went, in that very condition, straight to the prince, and related all that had happened. The prince was astounded at these words. Then the minister's son spoke, "Great prince! Feel no anxiety; you have not followed what it all implies."

Thereupon he said, "True; do you then explain it, that my mind may obtain rest."

He said, "In smearing camphor on the ten

fingers, and striking the woman on the face, she intimated that when the ten nights of moonlight will come to an end, she would meet you in the dark."

After ten days the old woman again went and announced him. Then the princess tinged three of her fingers with saffron, and struck them on the old woman's cheek, saying, "Get out of my house!"

After all, the old woman moved from thence in despair. She came and related the incident to the prince. He was plunged into an ocean of sorrow as soon as he heard it.

Seeing this state of his, the minister's son said again, "Be not alarmed, the purport of this matter is something else."

He replied, "My heart is disquieted; tell me quickly."

Then he said, "She is in the state which women are in every month, and hence has asked for three days more; on the fourth day she will send for you."

When the three days lapsed, the old woman called on the princess and made enquiries on behalf of the prince. Then she brought the old woman angrily to the western wicket, and turned her out.

Again the old woman came and informed the prince of this event. He became downcast on hearing of it.

On this the minister's son said, "The explanation

of the affair is simple- she has invited you tonight by way of that wicket."

The prince was pleased beyond measure on hearing this. When the hour arrived, they took out brown suits of clothes, arranged them, fastened on their turbans, dressed themselves, placed their weapons in order about them, and were ready. By this time midnight had passed. In the stillness of the night they, too, pursued their way in unbroken silence.

When they arrived near the wicket, the minister's son remained outside and the prince entered the wicket.

What did he perceive? The princess, too, standing there was expecting him. Thus their eyes met. Then the princess laughed, and, closing the wicket, took the prince with her into the festive chamber.

Having arrived there, the prince beheld censers filled with perfume burning in different parts of the room, and the maidens dressed in garments of various colours standing respectfully, with hands joined, each according to her station. On one side a couch of flowers was spread; attar-holders, pan-boxes, rose-water bottles, trays and four- partitioned boxes were arranged in order. On another side, compound essences, prepared sandal-wood, mixed perfumes, musk and saffron had been filled in metal cups. Here, coloured boxes of exquisite confections were laid out and there, sweetmeats of various kinds placed in order. All the doors and walls adorned with pictures and paintings displayed such faces that would enchant the beholder. In short, everything that could contribute to pleasure and enjoyment was got together. The whole scene was extraordinary of which no adequate description can be given.

Such was the apartment to which princess Padmavati brought the prince. Presently, she gave him a seat, and having his feet washed, applied sandal to his body. She then placed a garland of flowers round his neck, and sprinkling rose-water over him, began fanning him with her own hands. Upon this the prince said, "At the mere sight of you I have become refreshed. Why do you take so much trouble? It is not appropriate that these delicate hands should handle a fan; give me the fan; you be seated."

Padmavati replied, "Lord! You have been taking pains to come here for my sake; so, it is incumbent on me to wait upon you."

Then a maiden took the fan from the princess's hand and said, "This is my business; I will attend on you, and pray you both enjoy yourselves."

They began chewing betel-leaf together, and in familiar conversation, sat through the night till it became morning. The princess concealed him; and when night came they indulged in amorous pleasures. Thus several days passed away. Whenever the prince expressed a wish to depart, the princess would not permit him. A month passed; then the prince felt much disturbed, and very anxious.

Once it happened that the prince was sitting alone by night and thinking thus to himself, "Country, throne, family- everything had already been separated from me; but such a friend as mine, who has found me all this happiness, even him have I not met for a whole month! What will he feel in his heart? And how do I know what may be happening to him?"

He was occupied with such anxious thoughts when the princess arrived, and seeing his predicament, began to inquire, "Great prince! What grief possesses you that you are sitting so disspirited here? Tell me."

Then he replied, "I have a very dear friend, the son of the minister; for a whole month I have received no information of him: he is such a clever, learned friend, that through *his* talents I obtained you, and *he* it was who explained all your secrets."

The princess said, "Great prince! Your soul is really there; what happiness can you enjoy here? Hence, this is best – I will prepare confections and sweetmeats, and all kinds of meats, and have them sent to your generous companion. You will also go there and feast and comfort him well, and return with your mind at ease."

On hearing this, the prince rose and came forth; and the princess had different kinds of sweetmeats, with poison mixed, cooked and sent.

The prince had but just gone and sat beside the minister's son when the sweetmeats arrived.

The minister's son enquired, "Great prince! How did these sweetmeats come here?"

The prince replied, "I was sitting there anxious about you, when the princess came, and looking at me, asked, 'Why do you sit dejected? Explain the reason for it'. On this I gave her a full account of your skill in reading secrets. On hearing this account, she gave me permission to come to you and had these sent for you; if you will partake of them, my heart, too, will be rejoiced."

Then the minister's son said, "You have brought poison for me; it is well, indeed, that *you* did not eat of it. Sire! Listen to a word from me, – a woman has no love for her lover's friend: you did not act wisely in mentioning my name there."

Hearing this, the prince said, "You talk of such a thing as no one would ever do. If man have no fear of man, it is to be presumed he fears God at least."

With these words he took a round sweetmeat from among them and threw it to a dog. As soon as the dog ate it he fell dead on the spot.

The prince was enraged at seeing this turn of affairs, and began to say, "It is unbecoming to asssociate with so foul a woman; up to this hour her love has found place in my heart; now, however, it is all over."

On hearing this, the minister's son said, "What has happened has happened; you should now act in such a manner that you may be able to get her away to your home."

The prince said, "Brother! This, too, can be accomplished by you alone."

The minister's son said, "Today do this – go again to Padmavati, and do just what I tell you – first go and display much regard and affection for her; and when she falls asleep, take off her jewels, and strike her on the left thigh with this trident, and instantly come away from that place."

Having received these instructions, the prince went to Padmavati at night, and after much affectionate conversation, they both lay down together to sleep; but he was secretly awaiting his opportunity. When the princess fell asleep, he took off all her ornaments, struck her on the left thigh with the trident, and came to his own house.

He recounted all the occurrences to the minister's son, and laid the jewels before him. He then took up the jewels, took the prince with him, and assuming the guise of a *sadhu*, went and sat in a place for burning bodies. He himself took the part of a spiritual teacher, and making the prince his disciple, said to him, "Go into the market and sell these jewels; if anyone should seize you while doing this, bring him to me."

Receiving his instructions, the prince took the jewels with him to the city, and showed them to a goldsmith in close proximity to the king's palace-gate.

As soon as he saw them he recognised them, and said, "These are the princess's jewels; tell me truly, where did you get them?" He was saying this to him when ten or twenty more men gathered round. The *kotwal* hearing the news sent men and had the prince, together with the jewels and the goldsmith, arrested and brought before him, and inspecting the jewels, asked him to state truly where he had got them.

"My spiritual preceptor has given them to me to sell, but I know not whence he got them," replied the prince. Then the *kotwal* had the preceptor also apprehended and brought before him, and taking them both, together with the jewels, into the presence of the king, related all the circumstances.

On hearing the narrative the king addressed the *sadhu,* saying, "Master! whence did you obtain these jewels?"

The *sadhu* said, "Your majesty! On the fourteenth night of the dark lunar fortnight I visited a burning-ground to perfect some spells for a witch. When the witch came, I took off her jewels and apparel, and made the impression of a trident on her left thigh; in this way these ornaments came into my possession".

On hearing this statement from the *sadhu,* the king went into his private apartments, and the sadhu to his seat in the burning-ground.

The king said to the queen, "Just see if there is a mark on Padmavati's left thigh or not, and if so what sort of a mark there is."

The queen having gone and investigated, found the mark of a trident.

She returned to say, "Your majesty! There are three parallel marks; indeed, it appears as if some one had struck her with a trident."

On hearing this account, the king came out and sent for the *kotwal*, and told him to go and bring the *sadhu*.

The *kotwal* set off to bring the *sadhu* immediately on receiving the order; and the king began reflecting thus: "The affairs of one's household, and the intentions of one's heart, and any loss which has befallen one – these it is not right to disclose to anyone." In the meantime, the *kotwal* brought the *sadhu* into his presence.

Then the king took him aside and questioned him, saying, "Spritual guide! What punishment is laid down in the scriptures for an unworthy woman?"

On this the *sadhu* replied, "Your majesty! If a Brahman, a cow, a wife, a child, or any one dependent on us, be guilty of a disgraceful act, it is prescribed that the guilty should be banished from the country".

On hearing this the king had Padmavati conveyed away in a litter and left in a jungle.

Thereupon, both the prince and the minister's son started from their lodging on horseback, went to that jungle, took the princess Padmavati with them, and set out for their own country.

After some days, each reached his father's house.

The greatest joy took possession of all, high and low; and the prince and the princess, entered upon a life of mutual happiness.

After relating so much of the tale the Vetala asked King Vikramaditya. "To which of those four does guilt attach? If you do not decide this point, you will be cast into hell."

King Vikram said, "The guilt attaches to the king".

The Vetala asked, "How does the sin fall on the king?"

Vikram answered him thus: "The minister's son simply did his duty to his master; and the *kotwal* obeyed the king's command; and the princess attained her object; hence, the guilt falls on the king for having inconsiderately expelled her from the country."

On hearing these words from the king's mouth, the Vetala went and suspended himself on that same tree.

❒ ❒ ❒

2. MADHUMAVATI

On looking about him, the king perceived that the Vetala was not present; so he went back straightaway and, reaching that place, climbed up the tree, bound the corpse with the Vetala in it and placing him on his shoulders, set off.

Then the Vetala said: "O king! It is an irksome job you have undertaken. So, I will tell you another story to make you shake off your exhaustion."

On the bank of the Yamuna was a city named Dharmasthal, the king of which was named Gunadhip. A Brahman named Kesava lived there, who was in the habit of performing his devotions and religious duties on the banks of the Yamuna, and his daughter's name was Madhumavati. She was very beautiful. When she became marriageable, her mother, father and brother were all intent on getting her married.

It happened that while her father had gone one day, with one of his supporters, to a marriage ceremony somewhere, and her brother to his teacher's in the village, for instruction, in their absence a Brahman's son came to the house. Her mother, seeing the youth's beauty and excellent qualities, said "I will give my daughter in marriage to you." There, the Brahman had agreed to give his daughter to a young Brahman; whilst his son had given his word to a Brahman at the place where he had gone to study, that he would give him his sister.

After some days the father and son arrived with the two youths, and at home the third youth was awaiting them. One's name was Trivikram, the other's Vaman; the third's Madhusudan; they were all on a par in point of good looks, moral excellence, learning and age.

On seeing them, the Brahman began to reflect thus, "One girl, and three suitors-elect! To whom shall I give her, to whom not? — And we have all three given our words to the three of them. This is a strange piece of business. What shall I do?"

He was reflecting thus when in the meantime a snake bit the girl, and she died. On hearing the news, her father, brother, and the three youths, all five ran off in a body, and, after much toil and trouble, brought all the snake-charmers, conjurers, and as many magicians for the purpose of expelling poison.

They all looked at the girl and said she could not be restored to life. The first said, "A man bitten by a snake on the fifth, sixth, eighth, ninth, or fourteenth day of the lunar month does not survive." The second said, "One who has been bitten by a snake on the fifth, sixth, eighth, ninth, live." The third said, "Poison which has ascended into the system when the moon is in the fourth, tenth, ninth, sixteenth, nineteenth, and third asterisms of its path, does not descend." The fourth said, "One bitten on any of the following members, viz, an organ of sense, the lips, the cheek, the neck, the abdomen, or the navel, cannot escape." The fifth said, "In this instance even Brahma could not restore the dead to life; of what account are we then? Do you now perform her funeral rites; we are off." Having said thus, the conjurers went away; and the poor Brahman consequently took the corpse away, burnt it in the cremation ground and went off.

After he had gone, those three youths acted in this wise; one of them picked up and fastened together the charred bones of the burnt girl, and becoming a religious mendicant, went forth to wander from forest to forest. The second, having tied her ashes up in a bundle, built a hut, and began living on that very spot. The third became a devotee, furnished himself with a wallet and neck-band, and set out to wander from land to land.

One day he went to a Brahman's house in some country for food. The Brahman, on seeing him, began to say, "Very well; eat food here today."

On hearing this he sat down there. When the food was ready, he had his hands and feet washed, and took and seated him in the kitchen and himself sat down near him; and his wife came to serve the food.

Some was served, some remained, when her youngest son cried, and seized the border of his mother's saree. She persuaded him to let it go, but he would not; and however much she tried to soothe him, he cried all the more, and became more obstinate.

On this the Brahman's wife became angry, took up the child and threw him into the burning fire-place. The child was burnt to ashes.

When the guest witnessed this tragedy, he got up without eating anything.

Then the master of the house said, "Why do you not eat?"

He replied, "How can one partake of food in this house where a diabolical deed has been perpetrated?"

On hearing this the householder arose, and going to another part of his house, brought a book on the science of restoring the dead to life, took a charm from it, muttered some prayers, and brought his son back to life.

Then that Brahman youth seeing this wonder,

began to ponder, "If this book were to fall into my hands I, too, could restore my beloved to life."

Having made up his mind on this point, he ate the food, and remained there. Night came; in due course all partook of supper, and lay down in their respective places. Presently they were chatting together on one subject or another.

The Brahman youth, too, went and lay down apart, but kept awake. When he thought that the night was far advanced, and all had gone to sleep, he arose quietly, softly entered his host's room, took that book, and decamped; and in the course of several days he arrived at the place where the father had burnt his daughter. There he found the other two Brahmans also, sitting and conversing together. Those two also, recognising him, approached and met him, inquiring "Brother! You have wandered from land to land, it is true; but, tell us, have you learned any science as well?"

He said, "I have learned the science of restoring the dead to life."

As soon as they heard this, they said, "If you have learned this, restore our beloved to life."

He replied, "Make a heap of the ashes and bones, and I will restore your beloved to life."

They gathered together the ashes and bones. Then he took a charm out of the book, and muttered prayers; the girl rose up alive!

Thereupon Cupid so blinded the three of them that they began wrangling, among themselves.

Having related so much of the tale, the Vetala said, "O king! Tell me this; to whom did that woman by right belong? Or, whose wife was she?"

King Vikramaditya replied, "To him who built the hut and stayed there."

The ghoul said, "If he had not preserved the bones, how could she have been restored to life? And if the other had not returned instructed in the science, how could he have restored her to life?"

The king answered, "He who had preserved her bones, occupied the place of her son; and he who gave her life, became, as it were her father; hence, she became the wife of him who built a hut and remained there with the ashes."

On hearing this answer, the Vetala went again and suspended himself on that tree.

The king, too, arrived close at his heels, and, having bound him, and placed him on his shoulder. started off with him again.

❒ ❒ ❒

3. BIRBAR

There was a city, named Bardwan, wherein was a king named Rupsen. One day the king was seated in an apartment adjoining the gate of his palace, when, from outside the gate, loud voices of some people reached him.

The king asked, "Who is at the gate, and what noise is that?"

Upon this the gatekeeper replied, "Great king! You have asked a fine question! Knowing this to be the gate of a wealthy personage, persons of all kinds come and sit at it for the sake of money, and converse on a variety of topics; this is *their* noise."

On hearing this the king kept silent.

In the meanwhile a traveller, named Birbar, a Rajput, came from the south to the king's gate, in the hope of obtaining service.

The gatekeeper, after ascertaining his circumstances, said to the king, "Your majesty! An armed man has come in the hope of entering your service, and stands at the door; with your majesty's leave he may come before you,"

Having heard this, the king gave the order to bring him in. He went and brought him.

Then the king asked, "O Rajput! How much shall I allow thee for daily expenses?"

On hearing this, Birbar said, "Give me a thousand tolas of gold daily, and I shall be able to subsist."

The king enquired, "How many persons are dependant on you?"

He replied, "First, my wife, second, a son; third, a daughter; fourth, myself: there is no fifth person with me."

Hearing him speak thus, all the people of the king's court turned away their faces and began laughing; but the king began to consider why he had asked for a large sum of money. Ultimately he thought it out in his own mind, that a vast sum of money given away will some day prove of advantage. Coming to this conclusion, he sent for his treasurer and said, "Give this Birbar a thousand *tolas* of gold daily from my treasury."

On hearing this order, Birbar took a thousand *tolas* of gold for that day, and brought that gold to the place where he was staying, and dividing it into two parts, distributed one half among the Brahmans; and again dividing the remaining half into two parts, distributed one portion thereof among pilgrims, devotees, the worshippers of Vishnu, and religious mendicants; and of the one part which remained he had food cooked and fed the poor, and what remained over he consumed himself.

In this way he, with his wife and children, used regularly to subsist. And every night he used to take his sword and shield and go and mount guard over the king's couch; and when the king, roused from sleep, used to call out, "Is any one in waiting?" then he used to answer, "Birbar is in attendance; what may be your commands?" Thus answered he whenever the king called out, and thereupon, whatever the king ordered to be done, he executed.

In this way he used to keep awake the whole night long; nay, whether eating, drinking, sleeping, sitting still or moving about, that is to say, during the whole twenty-four hours he used to keep his lord in mind.

If one person sells another, this one becomes sold; but a servant, by entering service, sells himself; and, when sold, he becomes a dependant, and once dependant, he has no prospect of peace.

It is notorious, that however clever, wise and learned he may be, still when he is in his master's presence, he remains quite silent, like a dumb person, through fear.

So long as he is aloof from him, he is at rest. On this account it is that the learned say, "To perform the duties of a servant is more difficult than to perform religious duties".

One day the weeping voice of a woman chanced to come at night-time from the burning-ground.

On hearing it the king called out, "Is any one in waiting?"

Birbar instantly answered, "I am here; your commands."

Thereupon the king gave him this order, "Go to the spot whence the weeping voice of a woman proceeds, and enquire of her the cause of her weeping, and return quickly."

Having given him this order the king said to himself, "Whosoever desires to test his servant should order him to do things in season and out of season; If he executes his order, know that he is worth something; and if he objects, be sure that he is worthless. And in the same way prove brethren and friends in days of adversity, and a wife in poverty."

On receiving this order, Birbar took the direction whence the sound of the weeping proceeded; and the king also, after dressing himself in black, followed him secretly for the purpose of observing his courage.

In this interval Birbar arrived there. What does he behold in the burning-ground but a beautiful woman, lavishly decked with jewels from head to foot, crying aloud and bitterly!

At one moment she was dancing, at another leaping, at another running; and not a tear in her eyes! And while repeatedly beating her head, and crying out, "Alas! Alas!" she kept dashing herself on the ground.

Seeing her condition, Birbar asked, "Why art thou crying and beating thyself so violently? Who art thou and what trouble has befallen thee?"

On this she said, "I am the royal glory."

Birbar asked. "Why art thou weeping?"

Upon this she replied, "Impious acts are committed in the king's house, whence misfortune will find admission therein, and I shall depart thence; after the lapse of a month the king will suffer much affliction and die; this is the sorrow which makes me weep. Further, I have enjoyed great happiness in his house, and hence this regret: and this matter will in nowise prove false."

Birbar then asked, "Is there any remedy for it, whereby the king may escape, and live a hundred years?"

She replied, "Towards the east, at a distance of eight miles is a temple sacred to Devi; if you will cut off your son's head with your own hand, and offer it to that goddess, then the king will reign a hundred years precisely as he now reigns, and no harm of any kind will befall him."

As soon as he had heard these words, Birbar went home, and the king also followed him. Birbar awoke his wife and related the whole story to her.

On hearing the circumstances, she roused the son alone; but the daughter also awoke. Then that woman said to her boy, "Son! By sacrificing your head, the king's life will be saved, and the government, too, will endure."

When the boy heard this, he said, "Mother! In the first place, it is your command; in the second, it is for my lord's service; thirdly, if this body can be of use to a deity, nothing in the world is better than this for me; it is not right to delay any longer now in this business. There is a saying, 'If one have a son, to have him under control, – a body, free from disease, – science, such that one benefits thereby, – a prudent friend – a submissive wife – if these five things are obtainable by man, they are the bestowers of happiness and the averters of trouble: if a servant be unwilling, a king parsimonious, a friend insincere, and a wife disobedient, these four things are the banishers of peace and the promoters of misery."

Birbar again addressed his wife, "If thou wilt willingly give up thy child, I will take him away and sacrifice him for the king."

She replied, "I have no concern with son, daughter, brother, kinsfolk, mother, father, or any one, from you it is that my happiness proceeds, and in the moral code, too, it is thus written– 'A woman is purified neither by offerings nor by religious offices; her religion consists in serving and honouring her husband, no matter whether he be lame, maimed, dumb, deaf, blind, a leper, hunch-backed,– of whatever kind he be; if she perform any description of virtuous action in the world, while she does not obey her husband, she will fall into hell."

His son said, "Father! The man by whom his master's business is accomplished – his continuing to live in the world is attended with advantage; and in this there is advantage in both worlds."

Then his daughter asked, "If the mother give poison to the daughter, and the father sell the son, and the king seize everything, then whose protection shall we seek?"

The four, deliberating with one another somewhat in the above fashion, went to the temple of Devi. The king also secretly followed them.

When Birbar arrived there, he entered the temple, paid his adoration to Devi, and joined his hands in supplication, and said, "O Devi! Grant that, by the sacrificing of my son, the king may live a hundred years."

Saying this he struck such a blow with the sword that his son's head fell upon the ground.

On witnessing her brother's death, the daughter struck a blow with the sword on her own neck, so that her head and body fell asunder.

Seeing her son and daughter dead, Birbar's wife struck such a blow with the sword on her own neck, that her head was severed from her body.

Further, seeing the death of those three, Birbar, reflecting in his mind, began to say, "When my *son* is dead, for whose sake shall I continue in service? And to whom shall I give the gold I receive from the king?"

Having reflected thus, he struck such a blow with the sword on his own neck, that his head was severed from his body.

Beholding the death of these four, the king said to himself, "For my sake the lives of his family have perished: accursed is it any longer to govern a realm for which the whole family of one is destroyed, while one holds sovereignty; it is no virtue thus to reign."

Having deliberated thus, the king was on the point of killing himself with the sword; in the meantime, however, Devi came and seized his hand, and said, "Son! I am well pleased at thy courage, and will grant thee whatever boon thou mayest ask of me."

The king said, "Mother! If thou art pleased, restore all these four to life."

Devi replied, "That shall take place," and on the instant of saying it, Bhawani brought the water of life from the nether regions, and restored all four to life. After that the king bestowed half his kingdom on Birbar.

Having related so much, the ghoul said, "Blessed is the servant who did not grudge his life, and that of his family, for his master's sake! And happy is the king who showed no eagerness to cling to his dominion and his life. O king! I ask you this, – whose virtue, of those five, was the most excellent?"

Then king Vikramaditya replied, "The king's virtue was the greatest."

The ghoul asked, "Why?"

Then the king answered, "It behoves the servant to lay down his life for his master, for this is his duty; but since the king gave up his throne for the sake of his servant, and valued not his life as a straw, the king's merit was the superior".

Having heard these words, the ghoul again went and suspended himself on the tree in that burning-ground.

❑ ❑ ❑

4. THE MAINA'S STORY

The king, going to the tree again, bound the ghoul and took him away.

Then the ghoul said:

O king! There was a town named Bhogwati, of which Rupsen was the king, and he had a parrot named Churaman. One day the king asked the parrot, "What different things do you know?"

Then the parrot replied, "Your majesty! I know everything."

The king rejoined, "Tell me then, if you know where there is a beautiful maiden equal to me in rank."

Then the parrot said, "Your majesty! in the country of Magadh there is a king named Magadheshwar, and his daughter's name is Chandravati; you will be married to her. She is very beautiful and very learned."

On hearing these words from the parrot, the king summoned an astrologer named Chandrakant, and asked him, "To what maid shall I be married?"

He also, having made the discovery through his knowledge of astrology, said, "There is a maiden named Chandravati; you will be married to her."

Hearing these words, the king summoned a Brahman, and after explaining all, said to him at the moment of despatching him to king Magadheshwar, "If you return after finalising all arrangements for my marriage I will make you happy."

Heaving heard these words, the Brahman took leave.

Now, in the possession of Chandravati was a *maina,* whose name was Madanmanjari. The princess, too, one day asked Madanmanjari, "Where is there a husband worthy of me?"

On this the *maina* said, "Rupsen is the king of Bhogwati, he will be thy lord." To be brief, the one had become enamoured of the other.

In the course of a few days, the Brahman also arrived there, and delivered his own sovereign's message to that king. He too consented to his proposal, and summoning a Brahman of his own, entrusted to him the wedding gifts and all customary things, sent him along with that Brahman, and gave him this injunction, "Do you go and present my compliments to the king, and having marked his forehead with the usual unguento, return quickly: when you return I will make preparations for the wedding".

The two Brahmans set out thence. In the course of some days they arrived at King Rupsen's, and related all the occurrences at that place.

On hearing this the king was pleased, and after making all necessary preparations, set out to be married.

Reaching that country after some days, he married, and after receiving the bridal gifts and dowry, and bidding adieu to the king, started for his own kingdom. When leaving, the princess took Madanmanjari's cage with her.

After some days they arrived in their own country, and commenced living happily in their palace.

It happened one day that the cages of both the parrot and the *maina* were placed near the throne, and the king and queen entered into conversation, saying, "No one's life passes happily without a companion; hence it is best for us to marry the parrot and *maina* to one another, and put them both in one cage; then will they also live happily."

After conversing together thus, they had a large cage brought, and put both in it.

Some days after, when the king and queen were seated conversing with each other, the parrot began to talk to the *maina:* "Marriage is the essence of all bliss in the world; and he who, on being born into the world, has not enjoyed it, his life has been passed in vain. Hence, let me marry thee."

On hearing this the *maina* said, "I have no desire for a male."

Thereupon he inquired, "Why?"

The *maina* said, "The males are sinful, irreligious, deceitful and wife-killers."

Hearing this, the parrot said, "The females, too, are deceitful, false, stupid, avaricious creatures and murderesses."

When the two commenced wrangling in this manner, the king asked, "Why are you two quarrelling with each other?"

The *maina* replied, "Great king! All males are evil-doers and wife-killers, and hence I have no desire to have a male partner. Your majesty! I will tell you a tale, do you be pleased to hearken; for such are men."

* * * *

There was a city named Ilapur, and a merchant named Mahadhan dwelt there who could not get a family. On this account he was continually making pilgrimages and keeping fasts, and always hearing the *Puranas* read; and he used to give gifts profusely to the Brahmans. After some considerable time, by God's will, a son was born in that merchant's house. He celebrated the event with great pomp, and gave large gifts to Brahmans and bards, and also gave away a good deal to the hungry, thirsty and indigent.

When the boy reached the age of five years, he placed him in school for instruction. He used to leave home for the purpose of learning, but used to gamble with the boys when he got there.

After some time the merchant died, and the son becoming his own master, used to spend his days in gambling and his nights in fornication. Thus he dissipated his whole wealth in a few years, and having no alternative, quitted his country, and going from bad to worse, arrived at the city of Chandrapur.

In that place dwelt a merchant named Hemgupt, who possessed much wealth. He went to him, and mentioned his father's name and circumstances. The merchant felt instant pleasure on hearing these accounts; and rising and embracing him, inquired, "How came you here?"

Then he said, "I had engaged a vessel, and set out for an island to trade, and having arrived there and sold the goods, had taken in other goods as cargo, and left with the vessel for my own land; when suddenly so violent a storm arose that the ship was wrecked, and I was left seated on a plank; and so, drifting on, I have reached this shore. But I feel a sense of shame at having lost all my property and wealth. How can I now return and show my face to my fellow-citizens in this state?"

When he uttered such words in his presence, the merchant too began to think to himself, "God has relieved me of any anxiety without any effort of my own; now, a coincidence like this occurs through the mercy of God alone; it behoves me to make no delay now. The best thing to be done is to give my girl in marriage to him; whatever is done now is best; as for the morrow – who knows what it may bring!"

Forming this grand design in his mind, he came to his wife and began to say, "A merchant's son has arrived; if you approve, we will give Ratnavati in marriage to him."

She, too, was delighted on hearing this, and said, "When God brings about a coincidence like this, then alone does it occur; for the desire of our hearts has been fulfilled without our bestirring ourselves in the least; hence, it is best not to delay, but quickly send for the family priest, have the auspicious moment determined, and give her away in marriage."

Hereupon the merchant sent for the priest, had the fortunate *muhurat* determined, and gave his daughter away, bestowing a large dowry upon her. After marriage they commenced living together there.

After some days, the young man said to his bride, "A long time has passed since I arrived in your land, and no news of my household has reached me, and my mind remains troubled in consequence. I have told you my whole case; you should now so explain matters to your mother that she may, of her own free will, allow me to depart, that I may return to my own city. If it be your wish, do you also come."

On this, she said to her mother, "My husband desires permission to depart to his own land; do you, too, act in such a manner now that his mind may suffer no pain."

The merchant's wife went to her husband, and said, "Your son-in-law asks to return home."

On hearing this, the merchant said, "Very well; we will let him go, for we can exercise no authority over a stranger's son; we will do that alone wherein his pleasure consists."

Having said this, he sent for his daughter, and asked, "Will you go to your father in-law's or remain at your mother's? Speak your own mind."

At this she blushed, and gave no answer, but returned to her husband, and said, "My parents have declared that they will do that wherein your pleasure consists; don't you leave me behind."

The merchant summoned his son-in-law, loaded him with wealth, and sent him, and allowed his daughter to accompany him in a litter, together with a female servant.

When he reached a certain jungle, he said to the merchant's daughter, "There is great danger here; if you will take off your jewels and give them to me, I will fasten them round my waist; when we come to a town you can put them on again."

She no sooner heard this than she took off all her ornaments, and he having taken them, and sent away the bearers of the litter, killed the woman-servant and threw her into a well, and pushing his wife into a well also, went off to his own country with all the jewels.

In the meantime, a traveller came along that road, and hearing the sound of weeping, stopped, and began to say to himself, "How comes the weeping voice of a human being in this jungle?"

Having reflected thus, he proceeded in the direction of the sound of the crying, and perceived a well. On looking into it, what does he behold but a woman weeping! Then he took out the woman, and commenced questioning her on her circumstances, saying, "Who art thou, and how didst thou fall into this well?"

On hearing this, she said, "I am the daughter of Hemgupt, the merchant, and was accompanying my husband to his country, when thieves waylaid us, killed my servant and threw her into a well, and bound and carried off my husband together with my jewels. I have no intelligence of him, nor he of me."

When he heard this, the traveller took her along with him, and left her at the merchant's door.

She went to her parents. They at the sight of her, began enquiring, "What has happened to thee?"

She said, "Robbers came and plundered us on the road, and after killing the servant and casting her into a well, pushed me into a dry well, and bound and carried off my husband, together with my jewels. When they began demanding more money, he said to them, 'you have taken all I possessed, what have I now left?' Beyond this, whether they killed him or let him go, I have no knowledge."

Then her father said, "Daughter! feel no anxiety; thy husband lives, and God willing, will join thee in a few days for robbers take money, not life."

The merchant gave her other ornaments in place of all that had disappeared, and comforted and consoled her greatly. And the merchant's son, also, having reached home, and sold the jewels, spent his days and nights in the company of loose women, and in gambling, so much so that all his money was expended.

At last, when he began to suffer extreme misery, he one day bethought himself of going to his father-in-law's, and pretending that a grandson had been born to him, and that he had come to congratulate him on the event. Having determined on this in his mind, he set out.

In the course of several days he arrived there. When he was about to enter the house, his wife saw from the front that her husband was coming and said to herself, "He must not be allowed to turn back through any apprehension he may feel."

Upon this she approached him and said, "Husband! Be not at all troubled in mind; I have told my father that robbers came and killed my servant, and after making me take off all my jewels, and casting me into a well, bound and carried off my husband. Do you tell the same tale; feel no anxiety; the house is yours, and I am your slave."

After speaking thus she entered the house. He went to the merchant, who rose and embraced him, and questioned him on all that had befallen him. He related everything precisely as his wife had instructed him to do.

Rejoicing took place throughout the house. Then the merchant, after providing him with all that was needed for bathing, and placing food before him, and after ministering much comfort, said, "This house is yours, abide here in peace."

He commenced living there. After several days the merchant's daughter came and lay with him one night with her jewels on, and fell asleep. When it was midnight, he perceived that she had fallen into a sound sleep. He then inflicted such a wound on her neck, that she died; and after stripping her of all her jewels, he took the road to his own country.

* * * *

After narrating so much the *maina* said, "This your majesty, I saw with my own eyes. For this reason I have no wish to have anything to do with a male. You see, your majesty, what villains men are! Who would love a male, and so cherish a serpent in her own home? Will your majesty be pleased to consider this point, – What crime had that woman committed?"

Having heard this, the king said, "O parrot! Do you tell me what faults there are in women."

Thereupon the parrot started saying.

* * * *

There was a city called Kanchanpur, where dwelt a merchant, named Sagardatt, who had a son by name Shridatt.

The name of another city was Jayshripur, where there was a merchant, named Somadatt, and his daughter's name was Jayshri. She had married Shridatt who had gone to a certain country to trade. While he was away, she used to live at her parents' house.

When he had spent twelve years in trading, and she arrived at woman's estate here, she one day addressed a companion of hers thus: "Sister! my youth is being wasted; up to this moment I have tasted none of the world's joys."

On hearing these words, her companion said to her, "Be of good cheer! God willing, thy husband will soon come and join thee."

She got vexed at these words, and ascending to the upper chamber, and peeping through the lattice, saw a young man coming along. When he drew near her, his eyes and hers suddenly met. The hearts of both went forth to one another.

Then she said to her companion, "Bring that man to me."

On hearing this, the companion went and said to him, "Somadatt's daughter wishes to see you in private; but do you come to my house."

She then showed him the way to her house.

He said, "I will come at night."

The companion came and informed the merchant's daughter that he had promised to come at night.

When shc heard this, Jayshri said to her companion, "You go home; when he arrives let me know, and I will also come when free to leave home."

On hearing her words her companion went home, and seating herself at the door, began watching for his coming. In the meantime he arrived.

She seated him in the doorway, saying, "You sit here; I will go and announce your arrival."

She came to Jayshri and said, "Your sweet-heart has arrived."

On hearing this she said, "Wait a while; let the house-hold go to sleep, and then I will come."

And so, after some delay, when it was near midnight, and all had gone to sleep, she arose softly and accompanied her, and arrived there in a very short time; and the two met in her house without restraint. When nearly an hour and a half of night remained, she rose and returned home, and went quietly to sleep; and he also went to his house at daybreak.

Many days passed thus. At last her husband, too returned from foreign parts to his father-in – law's house.

When she beheld her husband she became troubled in mind and said to her companion, "Such is my anxiety, what shall I do? Whither shall I go? Sleep, hunger, thirst, all are forgotten; nothing is agreeable to me." And she told her the whole state of her heart.

She got through the day somehow or other; but at night, when her husband had finished supper, his mother-in-law had a bed made for him in a separate building, and sent word to him to go and take repose, while she said to her daughter, "You go and do your duty to your husband."

She turned up her nose and knitted her brows on hearing this and remained silent.

On this her mother rebuked her sharply, and sent her off to him.

Being powerless, she went there, but lay on the bed with her face turned away. The more he kept addressing her in words of tenderness, the more vexed would she become. On this he presented her with all the various descriptions of apparel, and the jewels which he had brought for her from different places, and said, "Wear these." Then, in truth, she became still more vexed, and frowned and turned her face away. And he, too, went to sleep in despair: for he was fatigued with the journey.

To her, however, thinking of her lover, sleep came not.

When she thought that he was in profound sleep, she arose softly, and leaving him asleep, went fearlessly in the dark night to the abode of her lover; and a thief seeing her on the way, thought to himself, "Where can this woman be going, alone, with her jewels on, at this midnight hour."

Thus soliloquising, he followed her. In short, she managed somehow to reach her lover's house.

Now, there, a snake had bitten and left him; he was lying dead. She thought he was sleeping. Being, as it was, consumed with the fire of separation, she hugged him without restraint, and began caressing him; and the thief from a distance was watching the fun.

An evil spirit, too, was seated on a pipal tree there, looking on at the scene. All at once it came into the mind of the spirit to enter his dead body and have carnal pleasure with her.

Having resolved on this, he entered the body, and after living with her, bit off her nose with his teeth, and went and sat on the same tree.

The thief observed all these occurrences. And she, in despair, went as she was, all stained with blood, to her companion, and related all that had happened. Her companion said, "Go quickly to thy husband ere yet the sun rise, and, weep aloud and bitterly. If any one should question thee, say, 'He has cut off my nose'."

She went thither instantly and commenced weeping and wailing excessively. Hearing the noise of her weeping, all her relations came, and lo! she had no nose, – was sitting noseless !

Then they exclaimed, "O you shameless, wicked, pitiless, mad wretch! Why have you bitten off her nose without any fault on her part?"

He, too, became alarmed on witnessing this farce, and began to say to himself, "Trust not a wanton-minded woman, a black snake, an armed man, an enemy, – and fear the wiles of a woman. What can an eminent poet not describe? What does he not know who has acquired supernatural power? What nonsense does a drunkard not chatter? What can a woman not accomplish? True it is, that the defects of horses, the thunder of the clouds, the wiles of woman, and the destiny of man, – these things even the gods do not comprehend; what power has man then to understand them?"

In the meantime her father gave information of the occurrence to the city magistrate.

Policemen came from the station there, and bound and brought him before the magistrate. The magistrate of the city gave notice to the king.

The king sent for him, and questioned him about the case, but he declared he knew nothing.

And on his summoning the merchant's daughter, and interrogating her, she replied, "Your majesty!

when you see plainly what has happened, why do you question me?"

Then the king put to him, "What punishment shall I inflict on thee?"

On hearing this, he replied, "Do unto me whatever you deem just."

The king said, "Away with him, and impale him!"

On receiving the king's order the people took him away to impale him.

Observe the coincidence; – that thief was also standing there, looking on at the scene.

When he was convinced that this man was about to be unjustly put to death, he raised a cry for justice.

The king summoned him, and asked, "Who art thou?"

He said, "Great king! I am a thief; and this man is innocent; his blood is about to be unjustly shed; you have not given judgment wisely."

Hereupon the king summoned the husband also, and questioned the thief, saying, "Declare the truth on thy honour! What are the facts of this case?"

The thief then gave a detailed account of the circumstances; and the king, too, comprehended them thoroughly. Ultimately he sent attendants, and had the woman's nose brought from the mouth of her lover, who was lying dead, and inspected it. Then he was assured that the man was guiltless, and the thief truthful.

Hereupon the thief said, "To cherish the good, and punish evil–doers, has from of old been a duty of kings."

After relating so much of the tale, the parrot Churaman said, "Great king! Such embodiments of crime are women! The king having had the woman's face blackened and her head shaved, had her mounted on an ass, and taken round the city, and then set at liberty; and after giving betel-leaf to the thief and the merchant's son, he allowed them to depart."

* * * *

Having related so much of the story, the ghoul said, "O king! To which of these two does greater guilt attach?"

King Vikramaditya said, "To the woman."

On this the ghoul asked, "How so?"

On hearing this, the king said, "However depraved a man may be, still some sense of right and wrong remains in him; but a woman does not give a thought to right and wrong; hence great guilt attached to the woman."

Hearing these words, the ghoul went again and hung himself on the same tree.

The king went again and took him down from the tree, tied him up in a bundle, placed him on his shoulder, and carried him away.

❒ ❒ ❒

5. THE ENVOY'S DAUGHTER

The ghoul started telling the following story.

There was a city named Ujjain, of which Mahabal was king. He had an envoy named Haridas, Haridas had a daughter by name Mahadevi.

She was extremely beautiful. When she became marriageable, her father thought he ought to seek a husband for her and give her in marriage.

The girl one day said to her father, "Father! Give me in marriage to some one who is possessed of all accomplishments."

Oh this, he said, "I will give thee to one who is acquainted with all sciences."

Subsequent to this, the king summoned Haridas one day and said, "In the south there is a king named Harichand; go and ask after his health and welfare for me, and bring me news thereof."

On receiving the king's command he took leave, and returning after some days, delivered to him the whole message of his royal master, and gradually took up his permanent abode near that monarch.

It happened one day that the king asked him "Haridas! Has the Kali era begun yet or not?"

On this he put his hands together and said, "Your majesty! We, are already in the Kali age; for, falsehood is rife in the world and truth lies slain; people utter soft words to one's face, while they harbour deceit in their hearts; virtue, has vanished; vice has increased; the earth has begun to yield less fruits; kings have begun levying and collecting taxes by force; Brahmans have become covetous; women have abandoned modesty; the son obeys not the father's command; brother trusts not brother; friendship has vanished from amongst friends; trust is no longer found in masters, and servants have cast aside their duty, and every description of impropriety meets the eye."

When he had said all this to the king, the king arose and went into the private apartments, and Haridas went and sat down in his own place.

In the meantime a Brahman youngster appeared before Haridas and prayed, "I have come to ask, a favour of you."

On hearing this, he, said, "What request have you to make? Mention it."

He replied, "Give me your daughter in marriage."

Haridas replied, "I will give her only to the most accomplished man."

Hearing this, he rejoined, "I am acquainted with all the sciences."

Then said the, envoy, "Show me something of thy knowledge; I shall then be able to judge."

Thereupon the Brahman youth said, "I have made a chariot which will convey you in a moment to any place you may wish to go to."

Then Haridas replied, "Bring it to me in the morning."

The youth brought the car to Haridas early in the morning. The two mounted the car, and arrived in the city of Ujjain.

It so happened that, prior to his arrival, another Brahman youth had come, and asked his eldest son, "Give me your sister in marriage;" and he also had replied, "I will give her to one who is learned in all the sciences;" and that Brahman youth, too, had said, "I am acquainted with all knowledge and science."

He had said, "To you will I give her."

A third Brahman youth had asked the girl's mother, "Give me your daughter." She, too, had given him the same answer; viz., "I will give my girl to him who is acquainted with all sciences." That Brahman's son also had replied, "I am acquainted with the whole body of science contained in the Shastras, and can shoot an arrow which will hit an object which is merely heard, and not seen." On hearing this, she, too, had said "I consent, and will give her to thee."

Haridas began to think to himself, "One girl and three suitors! To whom shall I give her, and to whom not?"

He was troubled by this thought, when a demon came at night and carried off the girl to the summit of a mountain in the Vindhya range. When morn arrived, and none of the household found the girl, they began to fancy all sorts of things; and the three suitors, too, on hearing of the matter came there.

One of them was a wise man, – him Haridas questioned, saying, "O wise man! tell me whither the girl has gone?"

He considered for a moment or so, and said, "A demon has carried off your daughter, and lodged her on a mountain."

On this, the second said, "I will kill the demon and bring her back."

The third said, "Mount my chariot and bring her back."

On the instant of hearing this, he mounted the chariot, reached the place, slew the demon, and forthwith brought her back.

And then they began quarrelling with one another.

Thereupon the father pondered over the matter in his mind, and said, "All of them have put obligations on me, to whom shall I give her, and to whom not?"

Having related so much of the story, the ghoul turned to Vikramaditya and asked, "Now, king Vikram! whose wife, out of the three, did the maiden become?"

He replied, "She became the wife of him who slew the demon and brought her back."

The ghoul said, "The good qualities of all were on a par– how came she to become his wife?"

The king replied, "The other two simply conferred favours, for which they were recompensed; but this one fought with and slew the demon and brought her away, hence she became his wife."

On hearing this the ghoul went again to the same tree, and suspended himself on it, and the king, too, went immediately, bound the ghoul, placed him on his shoulder, and carried him off as before.

❑ ❑ ❑

6. WASHERWOMAN'S DILEMMA

Again the ghoul said the following story:

O king! There was a city named Dharampur, of which Dharmshil was king and his minister's name was Andhak. He said one day to the king: "Your Majesty! Build a temple, and place an image of Devi therein, and pay constant adoration thereto, for this is said in the Shastra to possess great merit."

Thereupon the king built a temple and installed the image of Devi in it and began offering adoration after the manner prescribed by the Vedas. He would not drink water before worshipping.

When a considerable time had passed thus, the minister said one day, "Great king! The saying is well known that the house of sonless man is empty, a fool's mind is empty, and everything pertaining to an indigent person is empty."

On hearing these words, the king went to the temple of Devi, and joining his hands in supplication, began to extol her, saying, "O Devi! Brahma, Vishnu, Rudra and Indra await thy bidding and thou it was who didst seize the demons Mahishasur, Chand Mund, Raktbij and slaying the evil spirits, relieved the earth of its burden; and wheresoever trouble had befallen thy worshippers, there thou hast gone and aided them; and in this hope I have approached thy threshold; fulfil now the desire of my heart also."

When the king had uttered the praises of the goddess in this manner, a voice issued from the temple of Devi, saying, "King! I am well pleased with thee; ask any boon that thou may'st desire!

The king said, "Mother! If thou art pleased with me, grant me a son."

Devi replied, "King! Thou shalt have a son who shall be very powerful and very glorious."

Then the king made offerings of sandal, unbroken rice, flowers, incense, lights and consecrated food, and paid adoration. Moreover, he made it a practice of worshipping in this wise daily.

After some days, a son was born to the king. The king, with his family and kindred, proceeded with music and song, and worshipped at the shrine of Devi.

In the meantime, it happened one day that a washerman accompanied by a friend of his, was coming from a certain town towards this city, and the temple of Devi met his eye. He resolved on prostrating himself before the deity.

At that moment he beheld a washerman's daughter, who was very handsome, coming towards him. He was fascinated at the sight of her, and went to worship Devi.

After prostrating himself, he joined his hands in supplication and said in his heart, "O Devi!

If, through thy favour, my marriage to this beautiful girl should take place, I will give my head as an offering to thee."

After making this vow, and prostrating himself, he took his friend with him, and went to his own city.

When he arrived there, the separation from his lady love so troubled him that sleep, hunger, thirst– all were forgotten. He spent the whole day in thoughts of her.

On perceiving this woeful state of his, his friend went and told his father all the circumstances. His father also became alarmed on hearing these things, and reflecting on the matter began to say, "From observing his state it seems to me that if his betrothal to that maiden does not take place, he will grieve to death; wherefore it is better to marry him to the girl, that thus he may be saved."

Having thus considered, he took his son's friend with him, and on reaching that town, went to the girl's father and said, "I have come to solicit something of you; if you will grant my request, I will make it known." The other man replied, "If I possess the thing, I will give it; speak out."

Having secured his promise thus, he said, "Give your daughter in marriage to my son."

On hearing this, he too agreed to the proposal; and calling a priest fixed the day, the auspicious conjunction, and the moment of the marriage and said:

"Bring your son; I, for my part, will stain my daughter's hands yellow."

On hearing this, he arose, returned to his own house, got ready all the requisites for the marriage, and set out for the ceremony; and on reaching the place, and having the marriage ceremony performed, he took his son and daughter-in-law with him and returned home. The bride and bridegroom commenced a happy life together.

After some time, an occasion of rejoicing arose at the girl's father's and so an invitation came to the bride and bridegroom. The wife and husband got ready, and taking their friend with them, set out for that city.

When they arrived near the place, the temple of Devi came in the sight, and then his vow came to his mind. Thereupon he reflected and said to himself, "I am a great liar, and a very irreligious wretch, for I have lied to Devi Herself!"

Having said this to himself, he spoke to his friend, "Do you tarry here while I pay a visit to Devi."

And to his wife he said, "Thou also stay here."

Having said this he went to the temple, bathed in the pool, stood before Devi, joined his hands in supplication, addressed her reverentially and raised a sword and struck himself on the neck. His head was severed from his body, and fell upon the ground.'

Not seeing him for a very long while, his friend thought he ought to go and see what had happened; so he said to the wife, "Stay here; I will soon hunt him up and bring him here."

Having said this, he went into the temple of Devi, and lo! His friend's head was lying apart from his body! On beholding this state of things there, he began to say to himself, "The world is cruel. No one will suppose that he, with his own hand, offered his head as a sacrifice to Devi, on the contrary, they will say, that, as his wife was very beautiful, he (the friend), in order to possess her, killed him, and is practising this artful trick. Therefore it is preferable to die here; whereas to earn an evil reputation in the world is not desirable."

Having said this, he bathed in the pool, came into the presence of Devi, joined his hands and made obeisance, and taking up the sword, struck himself on the neck, so that his head was severed from his body.

And the wife, weary of standing there alone and watching for their return, became quite despaired and went in quest of them into the temple of Devi. Arriving there, what does she behold but the two lying dead! Then, seeing them both dead, she thought to herself, "People will not believe that these two have voluntarily offered themselves as sacrifices to Devi. Everybody will say that the widow was a wanton wretch, and that she killed them both and left them that she might indulge in her depravity. It is better to die than endure such infamy."

After reflecting thus, she plunged into the pool and bathed and coming into the presence of Devi, bowed her head in obeisance; then taking up the sword, was about to strike herself on the neck, when Devi descended from the altar, and came and seized her hand, and said, "Daughter! Ask a boon; I am well pleased with thee."

On this she said, "Mother! If thou art pleased with me, restore these two to life."

Then Devi said, "Unite their heads to their bodies."

In the tumult of her joy she changed the heads while putting them on. And Devi brought the water of life and sprinkled it upon them. The two rose up alive, and began disputing one with another; one saying, 'She is my wife': the other, 'She is mine.'

Having related so much of the story, the ghoul asked, "Now king Vikrama! Of which of these two is she the wife?"

The king replied, "Hearken! The guiding principle for this is laid down in the book of law: 'The Ganges is the best of rivers, and the Sumeru is the most splendid of mountains, and Kalpavriksh is the holiest of trees, and the head is supreme among all the members of the body'. According to this law, she becomes the wife of him who possesses the husband's head".

On hearing these words the ghoul went and again suspended himself on that tree: and the king having gone and bound him, placed him on his shoulder and carried him off.

❒ ❒ ❒

7. A KING IN QUANDARY

Said the ghoul:

O king! There was a city named Champapur, the king of which was Champakeshwar. And the queen's name was Sulochana, and the daughter's name Tribhuvan-sundari.

The princess was extremely beautiful; her face was like the moon, hair like black clouds, eyes like a gazelle's, eyebrows arched like a bow, nose like a parrot's beak, neck like a pigeon's, teeth like the grains of a pomegranate; the redness of her lips resembled that of the bimb, her waist was like a leopard's, hands and feet like the tender lotus, complexion like the champa flower; in short, the bloom of her youth was daily on the increase.

When she became marriageable, the king and queen began to feel anxious in their minds. And the news spread among the monarchs of the different countries round about that so beautiful a girl had been born in the palace of king Champakeshwar that, at a mere glance at her beauty, gods, men, and holy sages, would remain fascinated.

Thereupon, the kings of the different countries had their portraits painted, and sent by the hands of Brahmans to king Champakeshwar.

The king received them and showed them to his daughter, but none of them suited her fancy.

Thereupon the king said, "Do then make a public choice of a husband".

To this, too, she did not agree, but said to her father, "Father! Give me to him who possesses the three qualities of beauty, strength, and superior knowledge."

When several days had elapsed, four suitors came from four different countries.

Then the king said to them, "Do each of you set forth clearly before me the superior qualities and knowledge you possess."

One of them said, "I possess such knowledge that I manufacture a cloth and sell it for five rubies. When I realise the price, I give one of the rubies to Brahmans, of another I make an offering to the gods, a third I wear on my own person, a fourth I reserve for my wife, the fifth sell, and constantly support myself with the money so obtained. No one else possesses this knowledge. And as to the good looks I possess, they are open to view."

The second said, "I am acquainted with the languages of both land and aquatic beasts and birds; have no equal in strength; and my beauty is before you."

The third said, "So well do I comprehend the learned writings that no equal of mine exists; and my beauty is before your eyes."

The fourth said, "I stand alone in my knowledge

of the use of weapons; there is no one like me; I can shoot an arrow which will strike an object which is heard, but not seen; and my beauty is famous in the world, – you, too, must surely see it."

"On hearing the statements of the four of them, the king began to think to himself, "All four are on a par as to excellences; to which should I give the girl?"

Having reflected thus, he went to his daughter and set forth the virtues of all four of them, and asked, "To which of them shall I give thee in marriage?"

On hearing this, she hung down her head through modesty, and kept silent, making no answer.

After relating so much of the story, the ghoul said, "Now, King Vikram! For which of them is this woman suited?"

The king replied, "He who makes cloth and sells it is a *sudra* by caste; and he who knows the languages is a *vaisya* by caste; he who has studied the learned writings is a *Brahman;* and he who hits with an arrow an object which is simply heard, and not seen, is of *her* caste; the woman is suitable for him."

On hearing these words, the ghoul went again and hung himself on that tree; and the king, too, went thither, bound him, placed him on his shoulder, and carried him off.

❑ ❑ ❑

8. THE BELLE OF THE BEACH

The ghoul said; O king! There was a city named Mithalavati, the king of which was Gunadhip.

A young Rajput, named Chiramdeva, came from a distant land to enter his service. He used to go daily to pay his respects to the king, but did not obtain an interview.

In the course of a year he spent all the money he had brought with him while tarrying there without employment, and there in his native land, his home went to ruin.

It happened one day that the king mounted his horse for the chase, and Chiramdeva also joined his cavalcade.

The king became accidentally separated from his followers in a forest, and the attendants lost themselves in another jungle; Chiramdeva, however was following the king.

At length, he called out, and said, "Your majesty! All the attendants have remained behind, while I am accompanying you, making my horse keep pace with yours."

On hearing this, the king reined in his horse, and Chiramdeva came up to the king.

The king looked at him, and asked.

"How hast thou become so emaciated?"

He replied, "If I live with a master, who cherishes thousands of people, while he takes no thought of me, no blame attaches to him for this, but rather my own fate is to blame. As for example, by daylight the whole world is clearly visible; yet it is not visible to the owl; what blame can be imputed to the sun for this? It is astonishing to me that he who caused the means of subsistence to reach me in my mother's womb, should take no thought of me now, when I have been born, and am capable of enjoying worldly aliment. I know not whether he sleeps or is dead. And, in my opinion, it is better to swallow deadly poison and die, than ask for goods and money from a great man who, while giving the same, makes a wry face, and turns up his nose in contempt, and raises his brows. Now these six things render a man contemptible – first, the friendship of a perfidious man; second, causeless laughter; third, altercation with a woman; fourth, serving a bad master; fifth, riding a donkey; sixth, uncouth speech. And the following five things the Creator records in a man's destiny at the time of his birth–first, length of life; second, acts; third, wealth; fourth, knowledge; fifth, reputation. O king, so long as a man's virtues are conspicuous, all continue to be his servants; but when his virtues decrease, his very friends become his enemies. This one thing, however, is certain; by serving a good master one derives benefit sooner or later; he does not remain unbenefited."

On hearing this, the king pondered over all

these words, but did not then make any reply. He said this to him, however, "I feel hungry; bring me something to eat from somewhere."

Chiramdeva said, "Your majesty, bread is not to be obtained here."

Having said this, he went into the jungle, killed a deer, took out a flint and steel from his pocket, kindled a fire, boiled some slices of meat, and served up a plentiful meal to the king, and partook of it himself as well.

When the king was quite satisfied, he said, "Now, Rajput! Conduct me to the city, for the road is not known to me."

He conducted the king into the city, and brought him to his palace.

Then the king appointed him to an office, and bestowed many robes and jewels upon him. After that, he continued in close attendance upon the king.

One day the king sent the Rajput on some business to the sea-side. When he reached the seashore, he beheld a temple dedicated to Devi. He entered it, and worshipped Devi. But, on the instant of coming out thence, a beautiful damsel came up to him from behind, and began questioning him, saying, "O man! Why hast thou come here?"

He replied, "I have come in quest of pleasure, and at the sight of thy beauty I am fascinated."

She said, "If thou hast any design on me, first go and bathe in this pool; after that I will listen to whatever thou shalt say to me."

On the instant of hearing this, he took off his clothes, entered the pool and bathed, and came out, and lo! he was standing in his own city!

On beholding this marvel, he was filled with fear, and returning home in his helplessness, clothed himself, and went and related the whole story to the king.

The king no sooner heard it than he said, "Show me this wonder also."

This said, he ordered the horses, and both mounted and set off. After several days, they reached the seashore, and entered the same temple of Devi, and paid adoration.

When the king came out, the very same damsel, accompanied by a female friend, came and stood beside the king, and on beholding the king's handsome appearance, became fascinated, and said, "O king! I will execute any command you may give me."

The king replied, "If thou wilt obey my command, be the wife of my servant."

She said, "I have become the slave of thy beauty, how then can I become his wife?"

The king replied, "It was but this instant thou saidst to me, 'I will obey any command, you may give me.' No, carry out my command. Keep thy plighted word, and become the wife of my servant."

On hearing this, she said, "Your word is law to me."

Thereupon the king had his servant married

to her according to gandharva rites, and brought them both with him to his palace.

Having related so much of the story, the ghoul said, "Tell me, O king, of master and servant, whose was the greater virtue?"

The king said, "The servant's."

The ghoul asked again, "Was not the merit of the king greater, who obtained so beautiful a woman, and bestowed her on his servant?"

Thereupon king Vikramaditya said, "What superior merit is there in conferring favours, whose office it is to do so? But he who, while having his own interests to attend to, promotes the interests of another - he is the greater. For this reason, the servant's merit was the greater."

On hearing these words, the ghoul went and hung himself on that same tree; and the king went and again brought him down from thence, placed him on his shoulder, and carried him away.

❐ ❐ ❐

9. MADANSENA

Said the ghoul:

O king! There was a city named Madanpur, where lived a king named Birbar.

In that same country there was a merchant named Hiranyadatt, who had a daughter by name Madansena.

One day, in the spring-time, she went with her female friends, into her garden, to stroll about and enjoy the scene. It so happened that, previous to her coming out, Somdatt, the son of a merchant named Dharmadatt, had come, with a friend, to take stroll in the forest.

He came into that garden; and on beholding her became enamoured, and began to say to his friend, "Brother! Should she ever be united to me, then my living will be to some purpose; and if not, then my living in the world is in vain."

Addressing these words to his friend, and being distracted by the pangs of separation, he involuntarily approached her, and seizing her hand, began to say, "If thou wilt not love me, I will sacrifice my life on thy account."

She replied, "Act not thus; that would be a sin."

Then he said, "Thy amorous glances have pierced my heart, and the fire of separation from thee has consumed my body; my whole consciousness and understanding have been destroyed by this pain; and at this moment, through the overpowering influence of love, I have no regard for right or wrong; but if thou wilt give me thy word, new life will enter my soul."

She said, "On the fifth day from this day my marriage will take place; but I will first meet thee, and afterwards abide at my husband's."

After giving him this promise and taking her oath to keep it she departed to her home, and he to his.

On the fifth day her marriage took place. Her husband brought her to his home after the marriage.

After some days her sisters-in-law compelled her to go to her husband at night.

She entered his chamber, and sat quietly down in a corner. In the meantime, her husband seeing her, took her hand, and made her sit on the bed. As he was about to embrace her, she shook him off with her hand, and related to him all that she had promised the merchant's son.

On hearing this her husband said, "If thou really desirest to go to him, go."

Having received her husband's permission, she started for the merchant's place.

A thief seeing her on the road, came up to her in delight, and said, "Whither goest thou alone, at this midnight hour, in this pitch darkness bedecked with such garments and jewels?"

She replied, "To the place where my dearly beloved dwells."

On hearing this the thief said, "Who is thy protector here?"

She began to say, "Cupid, my protector, with his bow and arrows, is with me."

Having said this, she related her whole story to the thief, from beginning to end, and said, "Do not spoil my attire; I give thee my word that, when I return thence, I will deliver my jewels to thee."

On hearing this, the thief said to himself, "She leaves me, in truth, with a promise to deliver up her jewels to me; then why should I spoil her attire?" Thus reflecting, he let her go. He sat down there, while she went to the place where Somdatt was lying asleep.

She suddenly roused him as soon as she got there.

He arose bewildered, and commenced saying. "Art thou the daughter of a god, or sage, or serpent? Tell me truly who art thou? and whence art thou come to me?"

She replied, "I am the daughter of a man– the daughter of the merchant Hiranyadatt; Madansena is my name and dost thou not remember that thou didst forcibly seize my hand in the grove, and didst insist on my giving thee my oath; and I swore, at thy bidding, that I would leave the man I was married to and come to thee? I have come accordingly; do unto me whatever thou pleasant."

On this he asked, "Hast thou told this story to thy husband, or not?"

She replied, "I have mentioned the whole affair, and after hearing everything, he has allowed me to come to thee."

Somdatt said, "This matter is like jewels without apparel, or food without clarified butter, or singing out of tune– all these things are alike. Similarly, dirty garments mar beauty, bad food saps the strength, a wicked wife deprives life of its joy, a bad son ruins the family. Whereas a demon takes life on his being enraged, a woman, whether as a friend or a foe, is invariably the cause of sorrow. What a woman does not do is of little moment; for she does not give utterance to the thoughts of her mind; and what is at the tip of her tongue she does not reveal; and what she does, does not tell of. A wonderful creature has God created in the world in woman."

After uttering these words, the merchant's son answered her, saying. "I will have nothing to do with another's wife."

On hearing this she took her way back home again.

On the way she met the thief, and told him the whole story.

The thief, on hearing it, applauded her highly, and let her go.

She came nigh her husband and told him all the circumstances; but her husband evinced no affection for her, and said, "The beauty of the cuckoo consists in its note alone; a woman's beauty consists in her fidelity to her husband: and the beauty of an ugly man is his knowledge; the beauty of a devotee is his patient suffering."

Having related so much of the story, the ghoul asked, "O king! Whose is the highest merit of these three?"

King Vikramaditya replied, "The thief's merit is the greatest."

The ghoul asked, "How?"

The king replied, "Seeing her heart set on another man, her husband gave her up; through dread of the king, Somdatt let her alone; whereas there was no reason for the thief's leaving her unmolested. Hence the thief is the superior."

On hearing this, the ghoul went again and suspended himself on that tree; and the king also went there, took him down from the tree, bound and placed him on his shoulder, and once more carried him away.

❒ ❒ ❒

10. THE FAINTING QUEEN

The ghoul said:

O king! In the country of Gaud there was a city called Baradman, and the king of that place was named Gunshekhar.

His minister was a follower of the Jain persuasion, Abhaichand by name. Through his persuasion, the king, too, entered the pale of the Jain religion. He prohibited the worship of Shiva, as also that of Vishnu, and offerings of cattle, grants of land, oblations to deceased ancestors, gambling and intoxicating liquors – all these he interdicted; no one was allowed to practise them in the city, and no one could carry away bones to the Ganges.

The minister, too, with the king's sanction for these matters, had it proclaimed in the city that whoever performs these acts, the king will confiscate all his property, and inflict punishment on him and expel him from the city.

Thereafter the minister said one day to the king "Attend, O king, to an exposition of the sacred law: Whosoever takes the life of any one, this same takes his life also in another state of existence. It is on account of this sin that living and dying are inseparable from man on his entering this world. He is born again and again, and again he dies. Hence, it behoves man, on his being born into the world, to treasure up virtuous deeds. Observe how Brahma, Vishnu, Mahadeva, in one form or another, became incarnate in the world under the influence of love, anger, covetousness or infatuation!

"A cow, forsooth, is superior to them, for she is free from passion, hatred, pride, anger covetousness, infatuation; moreover she sustains the subjects. And the calves which are born to her also impart the utmost ease to the living things of the earth, and cherish them. It is for this reason that all the deities and holy sages hold the cow sacred.

"Therefore, to worship the gods, is not well: worship the cow in this world. And it is a duty to protect the life of every animal, from the elephant to the ant, including beasts, birds etc., up to man: there is no duty equal to that in the world. Those who add to their flesh by eating the flesh of other creatures, ultimately suffer the torments of hell. Hence it is incumbent on man to preserve life. Those who regard not the sufferings of others, but go on destroying the lives of other creatures, and eating them their lives are shortened on the earth, and they are born cripples, or lame, or blind of one eye, or blind of both eyes, or dwarfs, or hunch-backed, or with some such bodily defect. According to the limbs of beasts and birds which they devour, they eventually lose similar members of their own

"Further, the drinking of intoxicating liquors

is a great sin. Hence the consumption of flesh and intoxicating drinks is not right."

Thus unfolding to the king the wisdom stored up in his mind, the minister made him so sound a convert to the Jain faith, that whatever he advised the king did; and he paid no respect to any Brahman, ascetic, itinerant devotee, or religious mendicant, and governed his kingdom according to this religion.

One day, coming under the power of death, he died. Thereupon his son, Dharma-dhwaj by name ascended the throne, and began to reign.

One day, having had the minister, Abhaichand, seized, and seven plaits made of the hair on his head, and his face blackened, and the minister himself seated on a donkey, and a drum beaten and hands clapped in derision after him, he banished him from the kingdom, and carried on his government free from all anxiety.

One day, in the spring-time, the king, accompanied by his queens, went to take a stroll in a garden. There was a large tank in that garden, and the lotus was in full bloom there.

On beholding the beauty of the tank, the king stripped off his clothes, and went down to bathe. Having plucked a flower, and come to the side, he was handing it to one of the queens, when it slipped from his hand and fell on the queen's feet: and by the blow it inflicted, the queen's foot was broken.

On this the king became alarmed, and forthwith coming out from the tank, began applying remedies;

and in the meantime night came on, and the moon shone forth.

No sooner did the moon's beams fall, than blisters appeared on the body of the second queen.

Further, just then the sound of a wooden pestle from some householder's suddenly reached the third queen, and she was instantly attacked with so severe a headache that she fainted.

After narrating so much, the ghoul said, "O king ! Which of these three was the most delicate?"

The king replied, "The one who got the pain in the head and fainted away, she was the most delicate."

On hearing these words, the ghoul again went and suspended himself on that tree; and the king went there and took him down, and making a bundle of him, placed him on his shoulder and walked off with him.

❒ ❒ ❒

11. SUNDARI

The ghoul said:

Your majesty! There was a city named Punyapur, the king of which was Ballabh, and his minister Satyaprakash. The name of the minister's wife was Lakshmi.

One day the king said to his minister. "If one who is a king does not enjoy himself with beautiful women, vain is his sovereignty."

Having said this, and handing over the burden of the government to the minister, he himself gladly entered upon a course of amorous pleasures.

He abandoned all cares of the state, and commenced spending his days and nights in enjoyment.

It so happened that, one day, the minister was sitting dejected at home, when his wife asked him, "My lord! You seem to me to be very weak."

He replied saying, "Night and day the cares of government weigh heavily on me, and hence my body has become feeble; while the king is occupied the whole day long with his own pleasures and enjoyment."

The minister's wife said, "My lord! You have

carried on the government for a long time, now take leave of the king, and go on a pilgrimage for a few days."

He remained silent on hearing this speech of hers.

Afterwards, when he stirred out he went to the king when the king was holding his court, and, obtaining his permission to go on leave, set out on a pilgrimage.

Journeying on, he reached Rameshwar on the seacoast.

As soon as he arrived there, he visited the shrine of Mahadeva, and came out of the temple, when his gaze happening to stray towards the sea, what does he behold, but a marvellous tree of gold come up out of it, the leaves of which were emeralds, the blossoms topazes, the fruits corals. – it presented a most beautiful sight!

And seated on the tree was a very beautiful woman, holding a lute in her hands, and singing in most soft and sweet strains.

After a few minutes the tree disappeared in the ocean.

After beholding this spectacle there, the minister turned back and came to his own city, and, proceeding to the king, made obeisance, and joining his hands, said, "Your Majesty! I have witnessed a marvellous sight!"

The monarch said, "Describe it."

The minister said, "Your Majesty! Men of olden time have said that one should not speak of such things as are beyond the comprehension of any one, and which no one would credit. But this thing I saw plainly with my eyes, and hence I speak of it. Your majesty ! At the place where the Lord Raghunath had bridged the ocean, lo! a golden tree came up out of the sea, which was so splendidly loaded with emerald leaves, topaze flowers and coral fruits, that a description of it is impossible! And upon it was a very beautiful woman, with a lute in her hands, singing the sweetest of strains. But after a few minutes that tree was lost to sight in the ocean."

On hearing these words, the king entrusted the government to the minister, and set out alone for the seashore.

After several days he arrived there, and entered the temple to pay adoration to Mahadeva; and having bowed down and worshipped, he came out, when lo! The same tree, woman and all, rose out of sea.

As soon as the king saw her, her leaped into the sea, and went and sat on the same tree.

She, together with the king, descended to the nether regions.

She looked at the king and said, "Valiant man! Why hast thou come hither?"

The king replied, "I have come, attracted by thy beauty."

She rejoined, "If thou wilt not touch me during the dark fortnight of the lunar month, I will marry thee."

The king consented to this arrangement.

Notwithstanding this, however, she took the king's solemn promise, and then married him.

When the dark fortnight came, she said, "Your majesty should not remain near me today."

On hearing this, the king left her, taking his sword with him; and going apart, kept secret watch.

When it was midnight, a demon came, and, on the instant of arriving, folded her in his arms.

No sooner did the king witness this than he rushed forward with his sword, and said, "Foul fiend! Lay not thy hand on my wife before my eyes! First fight with me."

This said, he drew his sword, and struck such a blow that the head of the demon was severed from the body, and lay quivering on the ground.

On beholding this, she said, "O gallant man! Thou hast done me a great kindness!"

After saying this, she spoke again, "It is not every mountain that contains rubies, nor every city that holds true men, nor does the sandaltree grow in every forest, nor do pearls exist in the head of every elephant."

Thereupon the king enquired, "Why did this demon come to thee on the fourteenth night of the waning moon?"

She said, "My father is a Vidyadhara. Sundari is my name. Now it was an established custom for my father not to partake of food without me.

One day I was not at home at mealtime; thereupon, father became angry and pronounced a curse on me, saying, 'A demon will come and embrace thee every fourteenth night of the waning moon. On hearing this, I said, 'Father! You have indeed given me your curse; but now have mercy on me!' He replied, 'When an intrepid man shall come and slay that demon, thou wilt escape from this curse.' Now, therefore, I have escaped from that curse; and I will now go and pay my respects to my father."

The king said, "If thou appreciatest the kindness I have done thee, come at once and visit my dominions; after that, go and visit thy father."

She said, "Very well; I consent to what you say."

Thereupon the king brought her with him to his capital. Festive music and rejoicing began. The news spread throughout the city that the king had arrived. Then songs of congratulations and merry-making commenced in every house; and after that, all the musicians and singers of the city came and offered their congratulations at the court. The king gave away many presents, and performed many pious acts.

Again, after some days that fair one said, "Now, your majesty! I will go to my father's"

The king said in sadness, "Very well, go"

When she perceived the king to be sad, she said, "Your majesty! I will not go."

The king said, "Why hast thou given up the idea of going to thy father!"

She replied, "I have now become one of the human race, and my father is a demi-god; were I to go now, he would show me no respect; this is my reason for not going."

On hearing this the king was highly delighted, and gave away lacs of rupees in presents and religious offerings.

Hearing of these matters touching the king, the minister died broken-hearted.

Having told so much of the tale, the ghoul said, "O king! Why did the minister die?"

Then King Vikramaditya said, "The minister perceived that the king had taken to sensual enjoyments, and banished all the cares of government from his mind; that the subjects had lost their master; and so, no one would heed what he (the minister) said. This is the anxiety from which he died."

Having heard this, the ghoul went again and hung himself on that tree. The king went again, as on previous occasions, and placed him on his shoulder, and carried him away.

❒ ❒ ❒

12. LAVANYAVATI

O king Vir Vikramaditya! started the ghoul. There was a city named Churapur, where a king named Churaman ruled. His spiritual teacher's name was Devaswamin, who had a son named Hariswamin. He was as beautiful as Cupid, equalled Brihaspati in his knowledge of scientific and religious treatises, and was as wealthy as Kubera. He wedded and brought home a Brahman's daughter, whose name was Lavanyavati.

One night in the hot season they were both sleeping soundly on the flat roof of a summer house.

The woman's veil accidentally slipped off her face, while a demi-god was proceeding somewhere through the air in an aerial car.

His gaze suddenly fell upon her. He lowered the car, and lifting her upon the car without awakening her, flew off.

After some time, Hariswamin awoke, and lo! his wife was not beside him. On this he became alarmed, and coming down from thence, searched throughout the house. When he did not find her there either, he went about seeking her through all the streets and lanes of the city, but did not find her. Thereupon he began to say to himself, "Who has carried her off? and whither has she gone?"

When his efforts were of no avail, he returned home helpless and regretful, and searched for her there a second time, but did not find her.

The house appeared desolate to him without her, he lost all self-control in his disquietude and misery, and began crying out, "Oh darling of my soul! Oh, darling of my soul!"

Being exceedingly agitated by her separation from him, he gave up the position of a householder, renounced the world, girt a simple waist-cloth round him loins, rubbed the bibhuti on his body, put on a necklace of beads, and set out on a pilgrimage.

Proceeding on his pilgrimage from town to town, and village to village, he reached a certain town at midday.

Becoming extremely hungry, he made a cup-shaped vessel of the leaves of a dhak-tree, and carrying it to the house of a Brahman, asked, "Give me some food."

When a man comes under the influence of love he has no thought of duty, caste, or food; and regardless of everything, he eats food wherever he can obtain it.

When he begged alms of the Brahman, the Brahman took the cup-shaped vessel from him and entered the house, and brought it back to him filled with rice boiled in milk.

He took the cup, and came to the steps of a tank. There was a large banyan tree. He placed the rice-cup at the root of that tree and went to wash his face and hands in the tank.

A black snake came out from the roots of the tree, dipped its mouth into the cup and went away; and so the whole contents of the cup had become poisoned. Hariswamin did not notice it. In the meantime, he returned after washing his hands and face. He ate the rice and milk avidly, and the poison instantly entered his system.

When the venom started working, he realized his state and ran to the Brahman and accused him stating, "Thou hast given me poison, and I am now dying of it."

Having said so much, he reeled and fell dead. The Brahman, seeing the tragic end, became wild and turned his own wife out of the house, and said "Go thou hence, thou murderess of a Brahman!" thinking that she had mixed poison in the poor man's food.

Having told so much of the tale, the ghoul asked, "O king, to which of these does the guilt of killing Hariswamin attach?"

The king replied, "Poison exists in a snake's mouth as a matter of course; therefore no guilt attaches to it. Again, the Brahman gave him alms, because the other man was hungry; therefore guilt does not attach to him. The Brahman's wife had given him alms at the bidding of her husband; she, too, is without sin. And he ate the milk and rice unwittingly and hence he also is guiltless. In short, whoever imputes guilt to anyone of these, is himself a sinner."

On hearing this reply the ghoul went again and hung on to that tree, and the king also went there, and taking him down and binding him, placed him on his shoulder and carried him away from there.

❑ ❑ ❑

13. THUG AND THE DAMSEL

Said the ghoul:

O king! There was a city named Chandrahriday, and a king named Randhir ruled there. In the city, there was a merchant named Dharmadhwaja who had a daughter, by name Shobhani. She was very beautiful. In her prime of youth her beauty was each moment increasing.

It so happened that robberies became a nightly occurrence in that city. When the merchants experienced much vexation at the hands of the thieves, they all went to the king in a body and said, "Your majesty! Thieves have committed great outrage in the city; we can no longer dwell in the place."

The king replied, "Well, what has happened has happened, but henceforth you shall suffer no annoyance; I will take vigorous measures against them."

After saying this, the king summoned a number of watchmen and ordered them to keep guard, and directed them how to keep watch, and commanded them to slay the thieves wherever they found them, without asking any questions.

Guards began to keep watch over the city by night, and yet robberies continued to take place.

All the merchants proceeded in a body to the king, and said, "Your majesty has sent watchmen, and yet the thieves have not decreased in number and thefts occur daily"

The king replied, "You take your leave now; from tonight I will go forth to keep watch over the city."

On hearing this, they left the king, and went each to his own home.

When it was night, the king took his sword and shield, and, on foot and alone, began his watch over the city. Having advanced some distance in the course of his watch, and looked closely, he perceived a thief coming towards him.

On seeing him, the king called out, "Who art thou?"

He replied, "I am a thief: who art thou?"

The king said in reply, "I also am a thief."

He was pleased on hearing this, and said, "Let us commit a robbery together."

Settling this matter between them the king and the thief, conversing with one another, entered one of the quarters of the city and after committing thefts in several houses, carried off the articles and came to a well outside the city and having gone down into it, ultimately reached the chief city of the nether regions.

The thief stationed the king at the gate, and took the money and treasures to his own house.

In the meantime a woman-servant came out

of his house, and, seeing the king, began to say, "Your majesty! What a place you have come to with that miscreant! Well will it be if, ere he return, you fly hence as fast as you possibly can: otherwise he will kill you as soon as he arrives."

The king replied, "But I do not know the road! In which direction should I go?

Then the servant showed him the road, and the king came to his palace.

On the following day the king, with all his forces, went to the chief city of the nether regions by the road down the well, and surrounded the entire household of the thief: but the thief, escaping by some other road, went to the ruler of that city, who was a demon and said, "A king has led an attack against my house to kill me: at this moment, either you must aid me, or I will give up dwelling in your city, and take up my abode in some other place."

On hearing this, the demon said graciously, "You have supplied me with food: I am well pleased with you."

Having said this, the demon went where the king was with his army, surrounding the house, and began devouring the men and horses. And the king fled on beholding the form of the demon and all such as were able to run away, escaped and the rest the demon devoured.

The king was running off alone, when the thief came and cried out, "Art thou, a Rajput, flying from the battle?"

On the instant of hearing this, the king halted again, and the two confronted one another, and began to fight. At length the king overcame him, and bound his hands behind his back, and brought him into the city. After that, having him bathed and washed and clothed in fine apparel, and mounted on a camel, he sent him all round the city, accompanied by a crier and ordered the impaling stake to be erected for him. Whoever among the people of the city saw him said, "This same thief has plundered the whole city and the king will now impale him."

When the thief arrived near the house of the merchant Dharmadhwaja, the merchant's daughter hearing the sound of the crier's drum, asked her handmaid, "What is this proclamation about?"

She replied, "The king has brought captive the thief who used to commit robberies in the city. Now he will impale him."

On hearing this, she also came running to the lattice to see. No sooner did she behold the thief's comeliness and manly form than she became fascinated: and coming to her father begged, "Go to the king this moment, and return with that thief released."

The merchant protested, "How can you expect the king to release the thief who has robbed his whole city and on whose account his whole army has been destroyed?"

She again urged, "If you have to give up even all you possess to release him, bring him away free; and should he not come, I too will sacrifice my life."

On hearing this, the merchant went to the king and said, "Your majesty! Receive five lacs of rupees from me and set the thief at liberty."

The king replied, "This thief robbed the whole city, and my whole army was swallowed up through him. I will not on any account let him go."

When the king did not heed his request, he returned home in despair, and said to his daughter, "I said all that it was possible to say, but the king did not consent."

In the meantime, taking the thief round the city, they brought him to the impaling stake. The thief, hearing of the predicament of the merchant's daughter, first laughed aloud, and then wept bitterly. The people in the meanwhile pulled him on the stake.

The merchant's daughter, receiving intimation of his death, came to the same place to sacrifice herself to death for his sake.

She had a funeral pile erected, and sitting thereon, had the thief taken off the stake, placed his head on her lap, and quietly seated herself to be burnt. She was on the point of having the torch light it, when Devi instantly came out of her temple and said, "Daughter! I am pleased with thy courage: request a boon."

She asked "Mother! If you art pleased with me, restore this thief to life.

Thereupon the goddess said, "So shall it be."

Having said this, she brought nectar from the underworld and restored the thief to life.

Having told so much of the story, the ghoul inquired, "Say, O king! Why the thief first laughed, and why he wept afterwards?"

The king replied, "I know the reason why he laughed, and I know why he wept. Attend, O ghoul! the thief thought within himself: "Now that she is giving up all that she possesses to the king for my sake, what return can I make?" He wept at the thought of this. Again, however, he reflected: 'She loved me when I was about to die: the ways of God are inscrutable. He bestows wealth on the unlucky, knowledge on one of low origin, a beautiful wife on a fool, and He causes rain to fall in showers on the mountains.' Thinking of such things, he laughed."

On hearing this, the ghoul went again and hung on to that tree. The king went there, and unloosing him, made a bundle of him, placed him on his shoulder, and took him away.

❒ ❒ ❒

14. THE DILETTANTE LOVER

Attend, King Vikramaditya! There was a city named Kusumavati, of which one Subichar was king. His daughter's name was Chandraprabha.

When she became marriageable, she went out on one spring day, along with her companions, to stroll about in the garden.

Before the garden had been cleared of all strangers and others not permitted to set eyes on the women, a Brahman's son, named Manswi, of twenty years or so, very handsome, had come into the garden in the course of his wanderings, and had fallen in the cool shade under a tree asleep.

The king's attendants came and made arrangements for the ladies of the seraglio in the garden, but it so happened that none of them saw the Brahman's son sleeping there; and so he continued sleeping under that tree, and the princess entered the garden with her attendants.

Strolling about with her companions, where does she come but to the place where the Brahman's son was sleeping!

She no sooner arrived there than he also awoke at the sound of the people's footsteps.

The eyes of both met; and to such a degree did they come under Cupid's power that on the one side the Brahman's son fell upon the ground in a swoon, on the other, she too was so beside herself that her legs began to tremble.

Her companions, however, quickly laid hold of her on the very instant. At last, they laid her down in a litter and brought her home. And the Brahman's son was lying in so complete a state of insensibility there that he had no consciousness whatever of his body or mind.

During this interval two Brahmans, named Shashi and Muladeva, from the country of Kanvru, where they had studied the occult sciences, happened to pass by there. Muladeva, seeing the Brahman's son lying, said, "Shashi! How is it that he is lying in such utter unconsciousness?"

He replied, "A damsel has shot forth the arrows of her eyes from the bow of her eyebrows; hence he is lying insensible."

Muladeva said, "We ought to rouse him."

He replied, "What need is there for you to rouse him?"

He did not heed Shashi's words, but sprinkled water over him, and restored him to consciousness, and asked, "What has been the matter with thee?"

The Brahman said, "One should relate his troubles to him who can remove them; for what is to be gained by relating your sorrows to him who, on hearing of them, is unable to remove them?"

Muladeva said, "Well, tell me your troubles; I will remove them."

On hearing this, he said, " It was but now that the princess came here with her companions; and it was through seeing her that I had fallen into this state. Should I obtain her, I will preserve my life; otherwise I will abandon it."

Then Muladeva replied, "Come to my abode; I will exert myself to the utmost to obtain her; and, if I do not succeed, I will bestow great wealth upon thee."

Thereupon Manswi said, "God has created many a jewel in the world; but the jewel, woman, surpasses all; and for her sake it is that man treasures up wealth. When I have lost the woman, what shall I do with wealth? Beasts are better off in the world than those who do not possess handsome wives. The fruit of merits is wealth, and the advantage of wealth is ease, and the consequence of ease is taking a beautiful wife; now, what happiness can there be where there is no wife?"

On hearing this, Muladeva said, "I will give thee whatsoever thou may'st ask for."

Then he replied, 'O Brahman, obtain that same maiden's hand for me."

Muladeva thereupon said, "So be it; come along with me; I will have that very maiden bestowed on thee."

Ministering much comfort to him, he took him to his house; and when he reached there, he prepared two magic pills. One pill he gave to the young Brahman, saying, "When thou puttest this into thy mouth, thou wilt be turned into a girl of twelve years; and when thou takest it out of thy mouth, thou wilt become the self-same man thou wert before."

He said further, "Put this into thy mouth."

On his putting it into his mouth, he became a girl of twelve years. And Muladeva having put the other pill into his own mouth, became transformed into an old man of eighty years; and taking that young girl with him, he proceeded to the king.

The king, seeing the Brahman, saluted him, gave him a seat, and another to the young girl also. Then the Brahman gave him his blessing in verse, saying, "May He whose glory pervades the three worlds; and Who, taking the form of a dwarf, deceived King Bali; and Who, taking monkeys with Him, bridged the ocean; and Who, supporting the mountain (Govardhan) on his hand, protected the cowherds from the bolts of Indra, – may the same Vasudeva protect you!"

On hearing this, the king inquired, "Whence has your holiness come?"

The Brahman, Muladeva, replied, "I have come from the other side of the Ganges, and my home is there; and I had gone to bring my son's wife, and in my absence, a general flight from the village took place; and so I know not whither my wife and son have fled to. And now, with this girl with me, how shall I seek them? It is, therefore, advisable that I leave this girl with your majesty. Keep her with the greatest care until I return."

On hearing these words of the Brahman, the king began thinking to himself, "How shall I take charge of a very beautiful young woman? And if I do not take her, this Brahman will curse me, and my dominion will be overthrown."

Having thought this over in his mind, the king said, "Your holiness! The command you have given me shall be obeyed."

On this, the king summoned his daughter, and said, "Daughter! Take this Brahman's daughter-in–law and keep her with you, with all care and attention; and, whether sleeping or waking, eating or drinking, or moving about, do not let her be away from you for a moment."

On hearing this, the princess took hold of the hand of the Brahman's daughter-in– law , and led her away to her own apartment. At night, the two slept in one bed, and began conversing with each other.

In the course of conversation, the Brahman's daughter–in–law said, "Tell me, O princess! Owing to what trouble is it that you have become so worn and feeble?"

The princess said, "I went one day in the spring, accompanied by my female friends, to stroll about in the garden, and there beheld a very handsome, Cupidlike Brahman, and our eyes met. He swooned away on one side, and I became unconscious on the other. Then my companions, seeing my predicament, brought me home. And I am totally ignorant of both his name and his abode. His image fills my eyes, and I have not the least desire for food and drink. It is because of this trouble that my body has been reduced to the state you see."

On hearing this, the Brahman's daughter-in-law said, "What wilt thou give me if I bring thy beloved and thee together?"

The princess said, "I will remain thy slave for ever."

Hearing this, he took the magic pill out of his mouth and became a man again; and she was abashed at beholding him.

After that, the Brahman's son married her after the fashion of Gandharva marriages; and used constantly to convert himself thus into a man at night, and to remain a woman by day. At length, after six months, the princess became pregnant.

One day, the king went with his whole family to a marriage festival at his minister's house. There the minister's son beheld that Brahman's son disguised as a woman, and fell in love as soon as he saw her (or him), and began to say to a friend of his, "If this woman does not become mine, I will sacrifice my life."

In the interval, the king having partaken of the feast, returned to the palace with his family.

But the condition of the minister's son became most painful through the anguish of separation from his beloved, and he gave up food and water.

Seeing this state his friend went and informed the minister. And the minister, on hearing the story, went and said to the king, "Your majesty! Love for that Brahman's daughter-in-law has brought my son to a wretched state. He has given up eating and drinking. If you would kindly give the Brahman's daughter–in–law to me, his life would be saved."

On hearing this, the king said angrily, "Thou fool! It is not the nature of kings to do such a wrong. Hearken! Is it right to give away to another that which is given in trust, without the permission of the person making over the trust, that you mention this matter to me?"

On hearing this, the minister returned home in despair. Perceiving the suffering of his son, the minister also gave up meat and drink. When three days passed without the minister's eating and drinking, then, indeed, all the officials combined, and said to the king: "Your majesty! The minister's son is in a precarious state, and in the event of his dying, the minister, too, will not survive. And on the minister's dying, the affairs of the state will come to a stand–still. It is better that you consent to consider that which we state."

Hearing this, the king gave them permission to speak. Then one of them said, "Your majesty! It is long since that old Brahman left this country and he has not returned: God knows whether he is dead or alive. It is therefore right that you give that Brahman's daughter–in–law to the minister's son, and so uphold your kingdom: and should he return, you can give him villages and wealth. Should he not be satisfied with this, get his son married to another maiden and let him depart."

On hearing this, the king sent for the Brahman's daughter–in–law ,and said, "Go to the house of my minister's son."

She said, "The virtue of a woman is destroyed by her being gifted with excessive beauty, and a Brahman's character is lost by his serving a king and a cow is ruined by grazing in remote pastures, and wealth vanishes on meeting with abuse."

After saying so much, she added, "If your majesty would give me to the minister's son, settle this matter with him, viz., that he will do whatever I tell him; then will I go to his house."

The king said, "Say, what should he do?"

She replied, "Your majesty! I am a Brahman woman and he is a Kshatri by caste; hence it is best that he first perform all the prescribed pilgrimages, after that I will marry him."

When he heard this speech, the king sent for the minister's son and said to him, "First go and visit all the places of pilgrimage; after that I will give the Brahman's girl to thee."

On hearing these words from the king, the minister's son said, "Your majesty! Let her go and take up her abode in my house, and then I will go on pilgrimage."

After hearing this, the king said to the Brahman's girl, "If thou wilt first go and take up thy abode in his house, he will set out on pilgrimage."

Having no alternative, the Brahman's girl went at the king's bidding and took up her abode in his house. Then the minister's son was married to another girl; so he said to his wife, "Do you both live together in one place, on terms of the greatest affection and friendliness, and on no account quarrel and fight with each other, and never go to a stranger's house."

Having given them these instructions he for his part, set out on a pilgrimage; and at home his wife, whose name was Saubhagya–sundari, lying at night on one bed along with Brahman's daughter-in–law, began conversing on various topics.

After some time the wife of the minister's son spoke as follows:- "O friend! At this moment I am consumed with the flame of love; but how can my desire be attained?"

The other said, "If I accomplished thy desire, what wilt thou give me?"

She replied, "I will be thy humble and obedient slave for ever."

On this he took the magic pill out of his mouth and became transformed into a man. Thus he regularly transformed himself into a man by night, and into a woman by day. After that indeed, great love existed between the two of them.

In short, six months passed away in this manner, and the minister's son returned.

When people hearing of his arrival, began to rejoice the Brahman's daughter-in-law, having taken magic pill out of her mouth and transformed herself into a man came out from the house by way of the wicket, and went off.

After some time, he came to the same Brahman, Muladeva, who had given him the magic pill and told him his whole story from beginning to end.

Then Muladeva, after hearing all the circumstances, took the magic pill from him and gave it to his companion, Shashi, and each of them put a pill into his mouth. One was transformed into an old man, and the other a young man of twenty. After this the two went to the king's.

The king saluted them on the instant of seeing them, and gave them seats.

And they, too, gave the king their blessings.

After inquiring of their health and welfare, the king spake to Muladeva, saying, "Where have you been detained for so many days?

The Brahman replied, "Your majesty! I went to search for this son of mine, and having discovered him I have brought him to you. If you will now give up his wife, I will take both daughter-in-law and son home."

Then the king related the whole story to the Brahman.

The Brahman became very angry on hearing it, and said to the king, "What proceeding is this, for thee to give my son's wife to another? Well thou hast acted as thou pleasest; but now receive my curse."

Thereupon the king begged, “O holy man! Be not angry; I will do whatever you bid me”

The Brahman said, “So be it; if through fear of my curse, thou wilt do as I say, then give thy daughter in marriage to my son.”

On hearing this, the king summoned an astrologer, and after having the auspicious moment determined, gave his daughter in marriage to the Brahman’s son.

Then he took leave of the king and came to his own village, bringing the princess, together with her dowry, along with him.

On hearing this the Brahman Manswi also came there, and commenced quarrelling with him, saying, “Give me my wife.”

The Brahman named Shashi said, “I have married her before ten witnesses and brought her home; she is my wife.”

He replied, “She is with child by me: how can she become thy wife?”

And they went on wrangling with each other.

Muladeva reasoned much with both of them, but neither heeded what he said.

After relating so much of the story, the ghoul asked, “Say, king Vir Vikramaditya, whose wife was she?”

The king replied, "She became the wife of the Brahman Shashi."

Then the Ghoul asked, "Pregnant by the other Brahman, how could she become the wife of this one?"

The king replied, "No one was aware of her being with child by that Brahman; whereas this one married her in the presence of ten witnesses; therefore she became his wife. And the child, too will have the right to perform his funeral obsequies."

On hearing this, the Ghoul went and hung on to the same tree.

Again did the king go, and after binding the ghoul, and placing him on his shoulder, carry him away.

❑ ❑ ❑

15. JIMUTA-VAHAN

Said the ghoul:

O king! There is a mountain named Himachal, where there is a city of the demi-gods; and king Jimuta-ketu ruled there.

Once upon a time he worshipped Kalpa-vriksh a great deal for the sake of a son. Thereupon Kalpa-vriksh was pleased, and said, "I am pleased at perceiving thy services to me; ask any boon thou desirest."

The monarch replied, "Grant me a son so, that my kingdom and my name may endure." It said, "Even so shall it be."

After some time the king had a son. He experienced extreme joy, and celebrated the event with great éclat. After making numerous presents and charitable gifts, he summoned the priests and fixed a name for him.

The priests named him Jimuta-vahan.

When the child became twelve years of age he began to worship Shiva; and having completed the study of all the learned writings, became very intelligent, meditative, resolute, intrepid, and learned: there was no equal of his in those times.

And whoever came under his sway, were quickly alive to their respective duties.

When he attained manhood, he too, worshipped Kalpa–vriksh devoutly: whereupon Kalpa-vriksh was pleased, and said to him, "Ask whatsoever thou desirest, I will give it to thee."

On this, Jimuta-vahan replied, "If you are pleased with me, take away all poverty from my subjects, and let all those who dwell in my dominions become equal in point of possessions and riches."

When Kalpa-vriksh granted the boon, all became so well off by the possession of wealth, that no one would obey the order of any person, and no one would do work for any one.

When the subjects of that realm became such as has been described, brothers and kinsfolk of the king began to reason together, saying, "Both father and son are completely under the influence of religion, and the people do not obey their commands; it is therefore best to seize and imprison the pair of them, and take their kingdom from them."

The king unsuspectingly was not on his guard against them; and they having plotted together, went with an army and surrounded the king's palace.

When this news reached the old king, he said to his son, "What shall we do now?"

The prince said, "Your majesty! You be pleased to abide here in peace; I will go and destroy them this instant."

The king said, "O son! This body is frail, and riches, too, are unabiding; when a man is born, death too, attends him; hence we should now give up dominion, and practise religious duties. It is not right to commit a heinous sin for the sake of such a body, and for the sake of a kingdom, for even king Yudhisthira experienced remorse after his great war with the descendants of Bharat."

On hearing this, his son said, "So be it ! Make over the government to your kinsmen, and you yourself depart and practise religious austerities."

Having resolved on this, he summoned his brothers and nephews, and handed over the government to them. Father and son both ascended the mountain Malayachal, and on reaching the summit, built a hut and dwelt there.

In his new surroundings a friendship arose between Jimuta-vahan and a holy sage's son.

One day the king's son and the son of the sage went out together for a stroll on the top of the mountain. A temple, sacred to Bhawani, came in sight there. Within the temple, a princess, with a lute in her hands, was singing in front of the goddess. The eyes of the princess and those of Jimuta-vahan met, and both become smitten with love. But the princess, restraining her feelings, and stricken with shyness, turned her steps homeward; and he, too, for his part, being embarrassed by the presence of the sage's son came to his own place.

That night was passed by both the lovers in extreme restlessness.

As soon as morn came, the princess set out from her quarters for the temple of Devi, and the prince, too, starting from this side no sooner arrived than he perceived that the princess was there.

Then he asked her female companion, "Whose daughter is she?"

The companion said, "She is the daughter of king Malaya-ketu: her name is Malayavati, and she is a virgin as yet."

After saying this the companion spoke again and asked the prince, "Say, handsome man! Whence have you come and what is your name?"

He replied, "I am the son of the monarch of the demi-gods, whose name is Jimuta-ketu: and my name Jimuta-vahan. In consequence of our government having been overthrown, we, father and son, have come and taken up our abode here."

The companion, after hearing these words, related all to the princess.

She was much pained at heart on hearing them, and returned home; and at night she lay down with a load of care on her mind.

But her companion perceiving this state of hers, disclosed the story to her mother.

The queen, on hearing it, mentioned it to the king and said, "Your daughter has become marriageable; why do you not seek a husband for her?"

On hearing this, the king thought the matter over in his mind, and that very moment summoned his son Mitravasu, and said, "Son! Seek a husband for your sister and bring him here."

Then he spoke, "The king of the demi-gods, Jimuta-ketu by name, and his son Jimuta-vahan, abandoned their kingdom, and have come here to live." On hearing this king Malaya-ketu said, "I will give the girl to Jimuta-vahan."

Having said this, he bade his son go and bring Jimuta-vahan from the king's.

On receipt of the king's command, he set out for that house, and on, arriving there, said to the father, "Let your son accompany me, as my father has sent for him to bestow his daughter upon him."

On hearing this, king Jimuta-ketu sent his son along with him and he came to king Malaya-ketu's house.

Then King Malaya-ketu celebrated his marriage in gandharva fashion.

After the marriage, he brought his bride and Mitravasu with him to his own house. Then the three of them paid their respects to the king, and the king also gave them his blessing. Thus did that day pass.

On the morrow's morn, however, the two princes went out to take a walk on that mountain of Malayagir.

On reaching the place, what does Jimuta-vahan perceive but a very lofty heap of something white!

Thereupon he questioned his brother-in-law "Brother! How is it that this white heap is seen here?"

He replied, "Millions of young *nagas* come here from the infernal regions; the Garud comes and devours them ; this heap is composed of their bones."

On hearing this, Jimuta-vahan said to his brother-in-law, "Friend! You go home alone and take your food; for I always engage in worship at this hour, and the time for me to worship has now arrived."

On hearing this, he went; and Jimuta-vahan advanced further, when the sound of weeping began to reach him. Continuing his advance in the direction of the sound of the voice, he reached the spot; what does he behold but an old woman weeping with the burden of her trouble!

He went up to her and asked, "Why weepest thou, mother?"

Thereupon she said, "Today comes the turn of the serpent Sankhchur, who is my son; Garud will come and eat him up; it is on account of this grief that I weep."

He said, "O mother! Weep not; I will give up my life in lieu of thy son's."

The old woman said, "Pray do not do so! Thou art my son Sankhchur."

She was saying this, when, at that moment, Sankhchur arrived; and hearing her words, said, "Your Majesty! Worthless wretches like myself are born and die in vast numbers; but a just and compassionate being like you is not born everyday do not therefore, sacrifice your life for mine; for thousands of human beings will be benefited by your remaining alive; whereas it makes no difference whether I live or die."

Then Jimuta-vahan said, "It is not the way of true men to say that they will do a thing and then not do it. Go whence thou camest."

When he heard this, Sankhchur, for his part, went to pay adoration to Devi, and Garud descended from the sky.

In the meantime, the prince perceived that each leg of his was so long as four bamboos, and his beak was as long as a palm-tree, his belly like a mountain, his eyes like gates and his feathers like clouds.

All at once he rushed with open beak upon the prince. The first time the prince saved himself; but the second time he flew off with him in his beak, and began wheeling upwards in the air. While this was going on, a bracelet, on the jewel of which the prince's name was engraved, became unfastened, and fell, all covered with blood, before the princess.

She fell down in a swoon at the sight of it.

When, after a few minutes, she recovered her senses, she sent report of all that had happened to her father and mother. They came to her on hearing of this calamity, and on seeing the ornament covered with blood, burst into tears.

Now, the three of them set out in quest of him, and, on the road, Sankhchur too joined them; and advancing beyond them, went to the place where he had seen the prince, and began calling out repeatedly, "O Garud! Let him go! Let him go! he is not thy food. My name is Sankhchur. I am thy food."

On hearing this, Garud descended in alarm, and thought to himself, "I have eaten either a Brahman or a Kshatriya; what is this I have done!"

After this, he said to the prince, "O man! Tell me truly; why art thou giving up thy life?"

The prince replied, "O Garud! Trees cast their shade over others while they themselves stand in the sun, blossom and bear fruit for the benefit of others. Such is the character of good men and trees. What is the advantage of this body if it does not come of use to others? The saying is well known that, 'The more they rub sandal-wood, the more it gives out its perfume; and the more they go on peeling the sugarcane, and cutting it up into pieces, the more does its flavor increase; and the more they pass gold through the fire, the more surpassingly beautiful does it become.' Those who are noble do not give up their natural qualities even on losing their lives. What matters it whether men praise them or blame them? What matters it whether riches abide with them or not? What does it signify whether they die this moment, or after a length of time? The men who walk in the path of rectitude place not their feet in any other path, happen what may. What matters it whether they are fat or lean? In fact, his living is bootless whose body proves of no benefit to anyone; while those who live for the good of others their living is advantageous. To live for the mere sake of living is the way in which dogs and crows cherish life. Those who lay down their lives for the sake of a Brahman, a cow, a friend, or a wife, nay, more for the sake of a stranger, assuredly dwell in paradise for ever."

Garud said, "Everyone in the world cherishes his own life; and scarce, indeed, are those in the world who lay down their own lives to save the lives of others."

After saying this, Garud added, "Ask a boon; I am pleased with thy courage."

On hearing this, Jimuta-vahan said, "O god! If you are pleased with me, then henceforth eat no more serpents, and restore to live those you have eaten."

On hearing this, Garud brought the water of life from the infernal regions, and sprinkled it over the bones of the serpents, so that they rose up alive again.

Garud said to prince, "O Jimuta-vahan, by my favour thy lost kingdom will be restored to thee."

After granting this boon, Garud departed to his own abode, and Sankhchur also went home; and Jimuta-vahan too left the place, and met his father-in-law and mother-in-law and wife on the road. Then he came in their company to his father.

When they heard of these circumstances, his uncles and cousins, and indeed all his kinsfolk, came to visit him, and after falling at his feet imploring forgiveness, took him away, and placed him on the throne.

The ghoul asked "O king! Whose virtue was greatest among these?"

King Vikramaditya replied, "Sankhchur's."

"How so?" asked the ghoul.

The king said, "Sankhchur, who had gone away and so, got off safe, returned to give up his life, and save the prince from being eaten by Garud."

The ghoul said, "Why was not the virtue of him greatest, who laid down his life for another?"

The king replied, "Jimuta-vahan was a *Kshatriya* by caste. He was accustomed to holding his life in his hand, and hence he found it no hard matter to sacrifice his life."

On hearing this, the ghoul went again and hung on to that tree; and the king, having gone there and bound him, placed him on his shoulder, and carried him off.

❑ ❑ ❑

16. THE COMMANDER'S WIFE

The ghoul continued:

O King Vir Vikramaditya! There was a city named Chandrashekhar, and a merchant named Ratandatt was an inhabitant thereof. He had only one daughter, whose name was Unmadini.

When she attained womanhood, her father went to the king of the place, and said, "Your majesty! I have a daughter; if you desire to possess her, take her; otherwise I will give her to some one else."

When the king heard this, he summoned two or three old servants, and said to them, "Go and observe the appearance of the merchant's daughter."

They came to the merchant's house at the monarch's bidding, and all became fascinated at the sight of her beauty, – such beauty, as if a brilliant light was placed in a dark house; eyes like those of a gazelle; plaits of hair like female snakes; eyebrows like a bow; nose like a parrot's; a set of teeth like a string of pearls; lips like the bimb; throat like a set of a pigeon's; waist like the leopard's; hands and feet like a tender lotus; a face like the moon; complexion of the colour of the champa; a gait like that of a goose, and a voice like the cuckoo's; at the sight of her beauty the female divinities of Indra's paradise would feel abashed.

On beholding beauty of this kind, so abundantly rich in all graces, they decided among themselves saying, "If such a woman enters the king's household, the king will become her slave and will not give a thought to the affairs of the government. Hence, it is better to tell the king that she is ill favoured, and not worthy of him."

Having determined thus, they came thence to the king and gave the following account: "We have seen the girl; she is not worthy of you."

On hearing this, the king said to the merchant, "I will not wed her." Thereupon what does the merchant do on returning home but give Unmadini in marriage to one Balbhadra, who was the commander-in-chief of the king's army. She took up her abode in his house!

One day, the royal cavalcade passed by that way; and Unmadini too was standing, fully attired, on her house-top, at the moment; and her eyes and those of the monarch chanced to meet.

Then the king began to say to himself, "Is this the daughter of a god, or a female divinity, or the daughter of a human being?"

In short, he was fascinated at the sight of her beauty, and returned thence to his palace in a state of extreme agitation.

The warder, on beholding his countenance, said, "Your majesty! What bodily pain are you suffering from?"

The monarch replied, "While coming along the road today I saw a beautiful woman on a house-top. I know not whether she is houri, or a fairy, or a human being; but her beauty drove my mind distracted all at once; and hence I am agitated."

On hearing this, the door–keeper said, "Your majesty! She is the daughter of that same merchant who offered his daughter to you. Balbhadra, your majesty's commander-in-chief, has brought her home as his wife."

The king said, "Those whom I sent to examine her appearance have deceived me."

The king instantly ordered the mace-bearer to bring those persons before him without delay.

On receiving this order from the king, the mace-bearer went and brought them. In short, when they appeared before the king, his majesty thundered, "The errand on which I sent you, and that which was the desire of my heart – these things you failed to accomplish; on the contrary, you fabricated a false story, and gave it to me as an answer. Now, to-day, I have seen her with my own eyes. She is so beautiful a woman, rich in all distinguishing qualities, that it would be difficult to meet with her equal in these times."

On hearing this, they said, "What your majesty says is true; but graciously listen to the object we had in view in representing her to your majesty as ill–favoured. We decided among ourselves that, if so beautiful a woman enters the royal household, your majesty would become her slave on the instant of beholding her, and would neglect all the affairs of the State, and so the kingdom would go ruin. It was in consequence of this apprehension that we invented such a story, and laid it before you."

When he heard this, the king averred, "You speak the truth;" but he experienced the greatest uneasiness thinking of her.

Now, the king's distress of mind was known to every one, when, at the moment, Balbhadra, too, arrived, and putting his hands together in humble supplication stood before the king, and said, "O lord of the earth! I am your servant, she is your hand-maid, and you to suffer so much pain on her account! Be pleased, therefore, to give the order that she may be brought before you."

On hearing these words, the king said very angrily, "It is a grievous wrong to approach other's wife! What is this thou hast said to me? What! Am I a lawless wretch, that I should commit an infamous deed? The wife of another is as a mother, and the wealth of another is on a par with mud. Hear me, brother! As a man regards his own heart, so should he regard the hearts of others."

Balbhadra spoke again, saying "She is my servant. When I give her to your majesty, how can she any longer be the wife of another?"

The king replied, "I will not commit an act whereby reproach would attach to me in the world." The commander-in-chief said again, "Your majesty! I will turn her out of the house, and place her somewhere else, and after making a prostitute of her, will bring her to you." Thereupon the monarch said, "If thou makest a harlot of a virtuous woman I will punish thee severely."

After saying this, the king pined at the recollection of her, and, in the course of ten days, died. Then the commander-in-chief, Balbhadra, went and asked his spiritual teacher, "My master has died for the sake of Unmadini; what is right for me to do now? Favour me with your commands in this matter." He said, "It is the duty of a servant to give up his life also after his master's." This servant gladly went to the place where they had conveyed the king for cremation. During the time in which the king's funeral pile was got ready, he, too, did his ablutions and devotions; and when they lighted the pile, he too drew near the pile, and raising his joined hands to the sun, prayed, "O Sun-deity! in thought, word and deed, I solicit the gratification of this desire, viz., that at every successive birth I may meet with this same master, and for this hymn your praises." Having uttered this, he bowed in adoration, and leaped into the fire.

When Unmadini received this news, she went to her spiritual teacher, and telling him all, asked, "Your Holiness! What is the duty of a wife?" He replied, "It is by doing her duty to him to whom her father and mother have given her that she is termed a woman of good family; and it is thus written in the book of law that the woman who in her husband's lifetime practises austerities and fasting, shortens the life of her husband, and is finally cast into hell. But the best thing is this, that a woman by doing her duty to her husband, no matter how wanting he may be, secures her own salvation. Moreover, the woman who entertains the desire to sacrifice herself for her husband in the burning-ground, most undoubtedly derives as much benefit from as many steps as she takes towards this as would be derived from an equal number of horse-sacrifices. Further, there is no virtue equal to that of a woman's sacrificing herself for her husband on the funeral pyre." On hearing this, she made her salutation, and returned home; and after bathing, and performing her devotions, and giving large gifts to Brahmans, went to the funeral pile, and going once round to the right in adoration, said "O Lord! I am thy servant in each succeeding birth." Having said this, she, too, went and seated herself in the fire, and was consumed.

After relating so much of the story, the ghoul said, "O king! Whose virtue was greatest of these three?"

King Vir Vikramaditya replied, "The king's." The ghoul asked, "How so?" The king replied, "He left alone the wife given to him by the commander-in-chief, while he sacrificed his life on her account, and yet preserved his virtue. It behoves a servant to lay down his life for his master; and it is right for a wife to sacrifice herself for her lord. Therefore the virtue of the king was greatest."

Having heard these words, the ghoul went and hung on to that same tree. The king, too, followed him, and again bound him, and placed him on his shoulder, and carried him away.

❒ ❒ ❒

17. GUNAKAR

Said the ghoul:

Your majesty! There was a king of Ujjain, named Mahasain; and an inhabitant of that place was a Brahman, Devasharma, whose son's name was Gunakar.

This son turned to be a great gambler; and lost at play all the wealth the Brahman possessed.

Thereupon the members of the family turned Gunakar out of the house.

He could not help himself in any way; so having no other resource, he took his departure from the place, and in several days' time came to a certain city where he saw a devotee sitting over a fire, and inhaling smoke by way of penance!

After saluting him, he, too, sat down there.

The devotee asked him, "Wilt thou eat anything?"

Gunakar replied, "Your Holiness! Of course I will eat, if you give me something."

The devotee filled a human skull with food and brought it to him.

On seeing it he said, "I'll not eat food out of this skull."

When he did not partake of the food, the ascetic repeated an incantation, and a Yakshani appeared before him with joined hands and said, "Your Holiness! I will execute any command you may give me."

The ascetic said, "Give this Brahman whatever food he desires."

On hearing this, she built a very fine house, and furnishing it with all comforts, took him away with her from that place, and seating him on a cushioned chair placed various kinds of condiments and meats, by dishfuls, before him. He ate whatever he liked to his heart's content.

Again, after this, she placed the pan-box before him, and after rubbing down saffron and sandal in rose-water, applied the mixture to his body. Further, she clothed him in garments scented with sweet perfumes, threw a garland of flowers round his neck, and bringing him away thence, seated him on a bed.

Now while this was taking place it became evening, and she, too, having first decked herself out, went and sat on the bed, and the Brahman passed the whole night in her company

When morn arrived, the Yakshani went away to her own place, and Gunakar came to the devotee and said, "Master! She's gone away; what shall I do now?"

The ascetic said, "She came through the power of magic art, and abides near him who possesses the art."

He replied; "Impart this art to me, your Holiness, that I may practise it."

Then the devotee gave him a charm, and said, "Practise this charm for forty days, at midnight, sitting in water, and with a steadfast mind."

Thus he practised the charm, while many and various frightful objects appeared in view; but he felt no alarm at any of them.

When the time expired, he came to the ascetic and said, "Your Holiness! I come after practising the charm for the number of days you prescribed."

The ascetic now said, "Now practise it for the same number of days, sitting in fire."

He replied, "Master! I will go and pay a visit to my family, and then return and practise it."

After saying this, Gunakar took leave and went home; and when his relations saw him, they embraced him and commenced weeping; while his father said, "O Gunakar, where have you been so many days, and why did you forget your home! O my son, it is said that he who leaves a faithful wife and lives apart, and turns his back on a youthful woman or he who does not care for one who loves him, is on a level with the lowest of the low. It is said further that no virtue equals the domestic virtues, and no woman in the world imparts happiness equal to that which the mistress of one's house imparts; and those who slight their parents are impious men, and their future state will never, never be one of salvation; thus has Brahma declared."

On this Gunakar said, "This body is composed of flesh and blood, which is food for worms; and its nature is such that, if you neglect it for a day, a fetid smell proceeds from it. Fools are they who feel affection for such a body, and wise are they who set not their heart on it. Further, it is of the nature of this body that it is repeatedly born and destroyed. What reliance can one place on such a body! Cleanse it ever so much, it does not become clean; just as an earthen vessel, filled with filth, does not become clean by washing the outer surface; or however much one washes charcoal, it does not become white. Again, by what means can that body become clean, in which the fount of impurity is never-failing?"

"Whose father? Whose mother? Whose wife? Whose brother? The way of this world is such that numbers come and numbers depart. Those who offer sacrifices and burnt-offerings consider *Agni* their god; while those who are deficient in understanding make an image and worship it as god; but the class of ascetics regard god as in their very bodies. I will not practise such domestic duties as those you have mentioned, but will practise religious meditation."

Having said this, he bid adieu to his kindred, and practised the charm, sealed in fire. The Yakshani, however did not come.

Then he went to the ascetic who said to him, "Hast thou not acquired the art?"

Thereupon Gunakar said, "Just so, Master! I have not acquired it!"

Having related so much of the story the ghoul

asked King Vikramaditya, "Say, O king! Why did he not acquire the art?"

The king replied, saying, 'The practiser was of two minds, and did not give his undivided attention to the task, and hence he failed to acquire it. And it is said that a spell is perfected by the operator giving unwavering, single-minded devotion to it, and that he does not succeed if his thoughts are divided. Further, it is also said that those who are wanting in liberality do not obtain celebrity; and those who lack truthfulness are without shame; those who are wanting in justice do not acquire wealth; and those who lack meditation do not find God."

The ghoul asked, "How can the operator who sat in fire to work his spell be termed two-minded?"

The king replied, "When, at the time of practising the spell, he went to visit his family, the ascetic said to himself in vexation, 'Why did I teach the magic art to so vacillating an operator?' It was in consequence of this that he did not acquire the art. And it is said, that however much a man may exert himself, destiny attends him all the same; and whatever number of things he may achieve by force of his intellect, he, nevertheless, obtains that alone which fate has ordained."

On hearing this the ghoul went again and hung on that tree; and the king, too, followed him, and having bound him, and placed him on his shoulder, took him away.

❒ ❒ ❒

18. HARDATTA'S PROBLEM

The ghoul said:

Your majesty! There was a city named Kubalpur, the king of which was Sudakshi.

A merchant named Dhanakshi used also to live in that city, and he had a daughter whose name was Dhanvati. He gave her in marriage in her childhood to a merchant named Gauridatt. After a considerable time she had a girl, whom she named Mohani.

When she grew in years, her father died and the merchant's kinsfolk seized all his property. She, in her helplessness left the house in the darkness of the night, and taking her daughter with her, set out for the house of her parents.

After proceeding but a short distance, she lost the road, and came upon a burning-ground, where a thief was stretched upon an impaling stake. Her hand quite unexpectedly came in contact with his foot. He called out, "Who is it that put me to pain just now?"

On this she replied, "I have not willingly inflicted pain on you; forgive my fault."

He said, "No one gives either pain or pleasure to another; according as the Creator decrees one's fate shall be, so he experiences; and those who affirm that they did such and such things, are very unwise; for men are fixed to the cord of fate, which draws them after it whithersoever it pleases. The ways of the Creator are utterly inscrutable; for men propose a thing to themselves, and He brings something quite different to pass."

On hearing this, Dhanvati said, "O man! Who art thou?"

He replied, "I am a thief; this is my third day on the impaling stake and life will not quit the body."

She said, "For what reason?"

He replied, "I am unmarried; if thou wilt give me thy daughter in marriage, I will give thee ten million gold mohurs."

It is notorious that greediness is the root of all evil, pleasure the source of pain, and love the source of sorrow. Whoever keeps clear of these three lives happy. It is not every one, however, who can give them up.

Eventually, Dhanvati, through greed, became willing to give him her daughter, and asked, "It is my desire that thou shouldst have a son; but how can this be?"

He replied, "When she attains to womanhood, let her choose a young man and give him five hundred gold-mohurs, and ask her to live with him; thus will she have a son."

When she heard this, Dhanvati married the girl to him by giving her four turns round the stake.

Then the thief said to her, "There is a banyan tree near a large well of masonry to the east of this; the gold-mohurs lie buried beneath it; go thou and take them."

He said this, and died.

She went in the direction indicated, and on arriving there, took a few gold-mohurs from those buried, and came to her parents' house.

After relating her story to them, she brought them with her to her husband's land. Then she built a large house and began living in it; and the girl increased in stature daily.

When she became a woman, one day she stood with a female companion on the house-top casting her eyes upon the road. Just at that moment a young Brahman passed that way, and she, at the sight of him, was smitten with love for him and said to her friend, "O my friend! Bring this man to my mother."

On hearing this, she went and brought the Brahman to her mother.

She said, on seeing him, "O Brahman! My daughter is young; if thou wilt live with her, I will give thee a hundred gold–mohurs for a son."

On hearing this, he said, "I will do so."

Whilst they were conversing thus, evening came on. They gave him food to his mind, and he supped.

It is a well known saying that enjoyment is of eight kinds, perfume, woman, apparel, song, pan, food, the couch, and ornaments. All these existed there. To be brief, when the first watch of the night was nigh passed he repaired to the nuptial chamber, and spent the whole night in pleasure and enjoyment with her.

When it became morning, he went home, and she arose and came to her companions.

Then one of them enquired "Say! What pleasures did you enjoy with your love in the night?"

She replied, "When I went and sat near him, a kind of tremor made itself felt in my heart but when he smiled and took hold of my hand, I was quite overcome, and no consciousness of what took place remained to me. And it is said that if a husband be possessed of renown, is brave, clever, a chief, liberal, endowed with good qualities, a protector of his wife, then a wife never forgets such a man even in the world to come, much less in this world."

On that very night she conceived.

When the full time came, a boy was born.

On the sixth night, the girl saw in a vision an ascetic, with matted hair on his head, a shining moon on his forehead, ashes all rubbed over, wearing a while brahmimical thread, seated on a white lotus, wearing a necklace of white snakes, with a string of skulls thrown round his neck, and with a skull in one hand and a trident in the other, thus assuming a most awesome appearance, come before her, and say, "Tomorrow, at midnight, place a bag of one thousand gold-mohurs in a large basket, and enclosing this boy therein, leave it at the gate of the palace."

As soon as she heard this, her eyes opened;

And in the morning, she told all the circumstances to her mother.

When her mother heard this, she, on the following day, put the boy in a basket in the very manner directed, and left him at the king's gate.

At the palace the king saw an apparition with ten arms, five heads, each head having three eyes in it, and a moon upon it, very large teeth, a trident in hand – a most terrifying form, which came before him and said, "O king! A basket is placed at thy door; bring away the child that is in it; it is he who will maintain thy dominion."

As soon as the king heard this, his eyes opened. He then related the whole affair to the queen. After that, rising up thence, and coming to the door, he perceived the basket placed there. On the instance of opening the basket and peering into it, he beheld a boy and a bag of one thousand gold–mohurs in it.

He took up the child himself, and told the doorkeepers to bring in the bag. He then went into the harem and placed the child on the queen's lap.

By this time the day broke. The king came out, and summoning the sages and astrologers, questioned them saying, "Tell me, what marks of royalty are perceptible on this child?"

Thereupon one of the sages, who was acquainted with the science of interpreting the spots on the human body, spoke, "Your majesty! Three marks are distinctly perceived on this child; a broad chest, a high forehead; and a large face; in addition to these, your majesty! the whole thirty-two marks which are assigned to royalty exist in this one. Have no apprehensions on his account; he will rule over the kingdom."

On hearing this, the king was pleased, and taking off a chaplet of pearls from his own neck, presented it to that Brahman; and after giving large gifts to all the Brahmans; he bade them name the child.

Then the sages said, "Your majesty! Be pleased

to sit down with the queen fastened to you; let her majesty sit with the child in her lap; and summon all the musicians, singers, and others employed on festival occasions, and order rejoicings to take place; then will we give him a name after the manner prescribed by the sacred texts."

When the monarch heard this, he ordered his minister to do whatever they bade him.

The minister had rejoicings for the birth of the child forthwith proclaimed throughout the city.

On hearing this, all the professional rejoicers were in attendance, and congratulatory songs rang forth from every home; festive music began to strike in the king's palace, and rejoicings took place.

Then the king, and the queen with the child in her lap, came and sat within a square filled with coloured meal, perfumes, and sweetmeats, and the Brahmans began reciting the scriptures.

An astrologer having first determined the auspicious time, named the child Hardatt.

After that, he grew daily.

At length, at the age of nine years, he finished the study of the six shastras and fourteen sciences, and became a profound scholar. In the meantime, according to what was willed by God, his father and mother died. He ascended the throne, and began to govern justly.

After several years, the king one day thought to himself, "What have I done for my parents in return for being born in their family? The saying is that those who are compassionate, deal compassionately with all, they it is who are wise, and to them it is that Paradise is allotted. And the gifts, worship, religious penances, pilgrimages, and listening to the scriptures of those who are not pure of heart, is all in vain. And those who perform the funeral ceremonies and worship of the Manes without faith, and in pride, derive no advantage thereby, and so, their fathers go with their desires unfulfilled."

Reflecting in this manner, the king decided that he ought now to perform the funeral ceremonies of his fathers.

Thereupon King Hardatt proceeded to Gaya, and on arriving there, invoked the names of his fathers, and began offering oblations to them on the bank of the river Phalgu, when three hands came up out of the river.

He was troubled in mind on seeing this, wondering to which of the hands he should give the oblation and to which not.

Having reached this stage of the story, the ghoul asked, "O King Vikram! To which of the three was it right to give the oblations?"

Then the king said, "To the thief." The ghoul again asked, "For what reason?"

Thereupon the king said, "The seed of the lover had been bought; and the king took a thousand gold-mohurs and brought up the boy; and therefore neither of these two had any right to the oblation."

On hearing these words, the ghoul went again and hung on to that tree, and the king carried him away bound from thence.

❐ ❐ ❐

19. LAUGHTER AT DEATH

The ghoul continued:

O king! There was a city named Chitrakut, the king of which was Rupdatt.

One day he mounted his horse and went forth alone to hunt; and, having lost his way, got into a great forest. What does he see on going there but a large tank, in which lotuses were flowering, and various kinds of birds were sporting! On all four sides of the tank cool and perfume-laden breezes were blowing under the shade of the dense foliage of the trees. He, for his part, was overcome with the heat, so he tied his horse to a tree, and spread the saddle-cloth, and sat down.

A half-hour or so had passed when the daughter of a holy sage, very beautiful, and in the prime of youth, came to gather flowers.

Seeing her plucking the flowers, the king became deeply enamoured of her. When she was returning to her abode, after gathering the flowers, the king stood in her way and asked, "What conduct is this of yours, for you not to attend to me when I have come as a guest to your abode?"

On hearing this she stood still again. Then the king said, "They say that if one of low caste comes as a guest to the house of one of the highest caste, even he is entitled to respect; and whether he be a thief, or an outcast, or an enemy, or a parricide, – if even such a man comes to one's house, it is right to show him honour; for a guest is to be honoured more than anyone else."

When the king spoke thus, she stood still. Then, in truth, the two began to ogle at each other.

In the meantime the holy sage himself came up.

The king saluted on seeing him, and he in return blessed him, saying, "May you live long!"

Having said so much, he asked the king, "why have you come here?"

He replied, "Your Holiness! I have come a hunting." He said, "Why dost thou commit a great sin? It is said that one man commits a sin and many men reap the fruits thereof."

The king asked, "Your Holiness! Kindly favour me with your judgment of right and wrong."

Thereupon the sage said, "Attend, Your majesty! A great wrong is done in killing an animal that lives in the forest, supporting itself on grass and water; and it is a very meritorious act in man to cherish beasts and birds. It is said, moreover, that those who render unapprehensive the timid and refuge-seeking, receive the reward of those who are most liberal givers. It is also said that no religious austerity equals forbearance, and no happiness equals contentment, and no wealth equals friendship, and there is no virtue like mercy. Moreover, those men who are conscious of their duties, and show no pride on acquiring riches, accomplishments, learning, renown, or supremacy; and those who are content with their own wives, and are truth-speakers – such men obtain final salvation hereafter. And those who kill ascetics with matted hair, and without clothes and arms, experience the torments of hell at last. And the king who does not punish the oppressors of his subjects, he also experiences the torments of hell. And those who abuse a king's wife, or the wife or daughter of a friend, or a woman eight or nine months advanced in pregnancy – they are cast into the lowest and greatest hell of all. Thus is it declared in the book of law and religion."

On hearing this, the monarch said, "The sins which I have heretofore committed in ignorance are done, and are beyond recall: henceforth, God willing, I will not commit such again."

The holy sage was pleased to hear the king speak thus and said "I will grant thee any boon thou may'st ask for; I am highly pleased with thee."

Then the king spoke, "Your holiness! If you are pleased with me, give me your daughter."

When the sage heard this, he married his daughter to the king, after the manner of Gandharva marriage, and departed to his own place.

Then the king took the saint's daughter and set out for his capital.

On the road, about mid-way, the sun set and the moon rose.

Then the king, seeing a shady tree, alighted

beneath it, and tying the horse to its trunk, spread his saddle-covering and lay down along with her.

Thereupon, at the hour of midnight, a Brahman-devouring demon came and awoke the king, saying, "O king! I will devour thy wife."

The king said, "Act not so; whatever thou askest for I will grant."

Then the demon said, "O king! If thou wilt cut off the head of a Brahman's son seven years old, and give it to me with thine own hand, I will not eat her."

The king replied, "Even so will I do; but do come to me seven days hence in my capital, and I will give it thee."

Having bound the king by a promise thus, the demon departed to his own place; and on the morn arriving, the king also left and came to his palace.

The minister hearing of the king's arrival made great rejoicings, and came and presented gifts; and the king, after telling the minister of the adventure with the demon, asked, "Say, what means shall we adopt in the matter, for the demon will come on the seventh day?"

The minister said, "Your majesty! Feel no anxiety whatever; God will make it all right."

After saying so much, the minister had an image made of a maund and a quarter of gold and jewels studded therein, and had it placed on a cart, and conveyed away, and set up at a point where four roads met. He said to the keepers thereof, "If any persons come to look at this, say to them that any Brahman who will allow the king to cut off the head of a seven–year–old son of his may take possession of this."

Having said this, he came away. Thereupon the keepers used to speak of this to those who came to look at the image.

Two days passed away without any result. On the third day, however, a weak Brahman, who had three sons, hearing of this matter, came home and said to his wife, "If thou wilt give a son of thine to the king for a sacrifce, an image of a maund and a quarter of gold, and studded with jewels, will come into the house."

On hearing this, his wife said, "I will not give the youngest son."

The Brahman said, "The eldest I will not part with."

When the second son heard this, he said, "Father! Give me up."

He replied, "Very well."

Then the Brahman spoke again, "Wealth it is which is the source of all happiness in this world. Now, what happiness can reach him who lacks wealth? And if one be poor, his coming into the world is useless."

Having said this, he took the second son. and gave him up to the guards, and brought the image to his house; and the people, for their part, took the boy to the minister.

When seven days passed away, the demon came. The king took sandal, unbroken rice, flowers, perfumes, lamps, food for the deity, fruits and betel-leaf, and paid adoration to him; and, summoning the boy, took his sword in his hand, and stood ready to sacrifice him.

Thereupon the boy first laughed, and then wept.

While he was doing this, the king struck him a blow with the sword, so that his head was severed from his body.

True it is, as the sages have said: Woman is the source of misery in the world, the abode of imprudence, the destroyer of courage and the occasioner of infatuation, the bereaver of virtue. Who has pronounced such a source of venom to be the highest good? Again, it is said: Store up wealth against adversity, and disburse wealth to guard your wife, and give up wealth and wife to save your own life.

Having related so much of the story, the ghoul asked, "Your majesty! A man weeps at the moment of dying; will you account for this, Why did the boy laugh?"

The monarch replied, "He laughed at the thought of this, – viz., that in infancy a mother protects her child, and on his growing up, the father cherishes him; and in both good and bad times a king befriends his subjects,– such is the way of the world; whereas, my predicament is such that my father and mother have delivered me over to the king through greed of wealth, and he stands, sword in hand, ready to slay me, and the demon desires a sacrifice, no single one of them feels a spark of pity."

On hearing this, the ghoul went and hung on to that same tree; and the king also speedily arrived there and binding him, placed him on his shoulder, and carried him off.

❐ ❐ ❐

20. ABSENTEE HUSBAND

The ghoul said,

O king! There was a city named Bishalpur, the king of which was Bipuleshwar.

In this city lived a merchant whose name was Arthadatta, and his daughter's name was Anangamanjari. He had married her to a merchant of Kanwalpur, named Munni.

Some days after, the merchant crossed the ocean on a mercantile venture; and when she attained her womanhood at home she was standing one day in the pavilion, and observing what was going on in the road, when a Brahman's son named Kamalakar was coming along. The eyes of the pair met, and they became enamoured of each other at first sight.

After a quarter of an hour or so, recovering self-possession, the Brahman's son, in the restlessness consequent on separation from his beloved, proceeded to the house of his friend.

On her part Anangamanjari, too, was in extreme distress through the pain of separation from him, when, a female companion came and took her up; she had almost lost consciousness. Then the companion sprinkled rose–water over her and made her smell perfumes, and while so doing, her senses returned, and she said, "O Cupid! Mahadeva burnt thee to ashes, and yet thou wilt not desist from thy knavish tricks, but comest and inflictest pain on innocent, feeble women."

When she was uttering these words, it was evening and the moon appeared soon. Then she said, while gazing at the moonlight, "O moon! I used to be told that the water of life is in you, and that you shed it in your beams; to-day, however, even you have begun to pour down venom!"

She then said to her companion, "Take me up, and lead me away from this place, for I am being burnt to death by the moonlight."

Thereupon she raised her and took her to the pavilion, and said, "Dost thou feel no shame at uttering such words?"

Then she replied, "O friend! I am fully aware of all; but Cupid has wounded me, and rendered me void of shame, and I make great efforts to be patient, but the more I continue to be consumed with the fire of separation, the more venom-like does home appear to me."

The companion said, "Keep thy mind at ease; I will relieve thee of all thy suffering."

Having said this much, the companion went home; and she, love-lorn, determined in her mind that she would quit this body for his sake, and, being born again, enjoy life well with him.

With this longing in her mind, she threw a noose round her neck, and was about to draw it tight, when the companion arrived, and instantly taking the rope off her neck, said, "Everything can be attained by living, not by dying."

She replied, "Better is it to die than suffer such pain."

The companion said, "Repose awhile, and I will go and bring him.'

Having said this, she went to the place where Kamalakar lived, and taking a secret look at him, perceived that he also was much disturbed by the separation from his beloved, since his friend was rubbing down sandal in rose water and applying it to his body, and fanning him with tender leaves of the plantain–tree; despite which, he was crying out all aflame with passion and saying to his friend, "Bring me poison, I will sacrifice my life and be released from this suffering."

Observing this state of his, she said to herself, "However courageous, learned, sagacious, discreet and patient a man may be, Cupid reduces him to a state of distraction all the same."

These thoughts having passed through her mind, the companion said to him, "O Kamalakar! Anangamanjari has sent word to thee to come and bestow life on her."

He replied, "She, indeed, has given life to me."

After saying this, he rose up, and the companion went to the love-sick maiden, taking him along with her.

When he got there, lo! She was lying dead!

Thereupon he also uttered a cry of anguish, and therewith his spirit fled.

When it became morning, her household took both of them to the burning–ground, and arranging the pile, placed them thereon and set fire to it, when, in the meantime, her husband also arrived at the burning-ground, on his return from abroad!

Hearing the sound of the people's weeping, he went there, and what does he behold but his wife burning with a strange man!

He, also, being distracted with love, burnt himself to death in the same fire.

The people of the city, hearing this intelligence, began saying one to another, "Neither has eye seen, nor ear heard of so wonderful an event!"

After relating so much of the story, the ghoul asked "O king! Whose love, of these three, was greatest?"

The king said, "Her husband was the deepest lover."

"Why?" questioned the ghoul.

The king replied, "He who, on seeing his wife dead for another's sake, put aside anger, and cheerfully laid down his life through love for her – he is the deepest lover."

Hearing these words, the ghoul went again and hung on to that tree. The king, too, went there, bound him, placed him on his shoulder, and carried him off.

❑❑❑

21. THE GREATEST FOOL

The ghoul said;

Your majesty! There was a city named Jaysthal the king of which was named Varddhaman. In this city was a Brahman named Vishnuswami, who had four sons; one a gambler, the second a lover of women, the third a fornicator and the fourth an atheist.

The Brahman was one day admonishing his sons, saying, "Wealth abides not in the house of him who gambles."

The gambler became greatly annoyed at hearing this. And the father spoke again, "It is said in the *Rajniti* (or book of policy), 'Cut off the nose and ears of a gambler, and expel him from the land, so that others may not gamble; and although the gambler may have a wife and family in his house, do not consider them as in the house, for there's no knowing when he may lose them at play.'

"Again, those who are attracted by the wiles of courtesans purchase suffering for their own souls, while they part with their all under the influence of harlots, and take to stealing in the end. It is said, further, that wise men keep far away from such women as ensnare their hearts in a moment; whereas the unwise give up their hearts and so lose all their honesty, good disposition, reputation, conduct, judgment, piety, and moral character.

"Moreover, the exhortation of their spiritual preceptors is unpalatable to them. It is also said that when one has lost his own sense of shame, why should he fear to dishonour any one else? And there is a proverb to the effect: When will the cat that devours its own kitten allow a rat to escape!"

He went on to say, "Those who do not acquire knowledge in their childhood, and who on attaining manhood become engrossed in amorous pleasures, and continue to pride themselves on their youth, – those persons, in their old age, are consumed with regretful longings for that which they have neglected in their youth."

On hearing these words, all four of them came to the collective decision that it was better for an ignorant man to die than live; and hence, it was best for them to visit some other land and study science.

Determining on this, they went to another city, and after some time, having studied and become learned, they set out for their home. What do they see on the road but a Kanjar, who, after skinning and cutting up a dead tiger, and making a bundle of its bones, was about to take them away! Thereupon they said to one another, "Come, let each of us put his knowledge to the proof."

Having determined on this, one of them called

the Kanjar and gave him something, and taking the bundle, sent him away; and, quitting the road, they opened the bundle. One of them arranged all the bones in their proper places, repeated an incantation and sprinkled something over them, so that they became united.

In the same way the second brought the flesh together on the bones. The third, in the same manner, fixed the skin on the flesh. The fourth, in the same way, raised it to life. Thereupon it devoured the whole four of them as soon as it arose.

After reaching this point of the story, the ghoul asked, "Your Majesty! Who was the greatest fool of those four?

King Vikram replied, "He who restored it to life was the greatest fool. And it is said that knowledge without wisdom is of no use whatever; on the contrary, wisdom is superior to learning; and those who lack wisdom die just as he who raised the tiger to life died."

When the ghoul heard these words, he went and suspended himself on that same tree. Again did the king bind him, place him on his shoulder, and carry him away as before.

❑ ❑ ❑

22. TRANSMIGRATION

Continued the ghoul;

Your majesty! There was a city named Biswapur, the king of which was named Bidagdha. A Brahman, named Narayan, dwelt in that city. He one day began thinking to himself, "My body has become old, and I am acquainted with the science which enables one to enter another's body, it is therefore better that I quit this old body, and enter the body of some young man and enjoy life."

When he had determined on this in his mind, he set about entering a youthful body; but first he wept, and then he laughed, and after that he entered it and came home.

All his kinsfolk, however, were aware of what he had done, and thereupon he said to them, "I have now become an ascetic."

Having said this, he began to recite as follows: "He who dries up the fountain of hope with the fire of austere devotion, and placing his soul therein, deadens his senses may be termed a wise devotee. But the way of the people of this world is such, that the body may waste away, the head shake, the teeth drop out, and they walk about with a stick in their old age, yet even then, desire is not quenched. And thus it is that time passes away–day comes, night arrives, a month is over, a year is completed; one is a child, then an old man, while nothing is known as to who one and who others are, and why one grieves for another.

"One comes, another goes, and ultimately all life must depart — not one of these will remain. Many and various bodies are there, and many and various minds, and many and various affections, and various kinds of delusions has Brahma created; but the wise escape these, and quenching hope and desire, shaving their heads, taking a staff and water-pot in their hands, subduing the passions of love and anger, become ascetics; and wander barefooted from one place of pilgrimage to another; these same find eternal salvation.

"This world, moreover, is as a dream; to whom can you impart pleasure in it, to whom pain? It is even like the new leaf shooting from the centre of the plantain tree, wherein is no pith whatever. And those who pride themselves on riches, youth, or knowledge, are unwise. Again, they who turn devotees, and taking a water-pot in hand, beg alms from door to door, and nourishing their bodies with milk, clarified butter, and sugar, become lustful, and thereby immoral; they nullify their religious meditations."

After repeating so much, he proceeded, saying, "I will now go on a pilgrimage."

On hearing these words, his relations were very pleased.

Having told so much of the story, the ghoul asked, "Your majesty! Why did he weep, and why did he laugh?"

Then the king replied, "Calling to mind his mother's love in his infancy, and the happiness of his youth, and from a feeling of affection in having remained so many days in that body, he wept; and having succeeded in his art, and entered a new body; he laughed with pleasure."

On hearing these words, the ghoul went and hung on to the same tree; and again did the king bind him as before, place him on his shoulder, and carry him away.

❐ ❐ ❐

23. CONNOISSEUR PAR EXCELLENCE

The ghoul said:

Your majesty! There was a city named Dharampur, where a king named Dharmaj ruled. In this city was a Brahman named Govind, versed in all the four Vedas and all the six learned sastras, and a careful observer of all his religious duties; and Haridatt, Somdatt, Yagyadatt and Brahmadatt were his four sons. They were very learned, very clever, and at all times obedient to their father.

After some time his eldest son died, and he, too, was at the point of death through grief for him.

At that time, Vishnusharma, the king's family priest, came and began reasoning with him, saying, "When this being, man, enters the mother's womb, he first suffers pain there; secondly falling under the influence of love in youth, he endures the anguish of separation from his beloved; thirdly, becoming old, he is involved in suffering through his body being feeble. In brief, many are the sorrows attendant on being born in the world, and few are the joys; for, the world is the source of sorrow.

"If a man were to climb to the top of a tree, or go and sit on the summit of a mountain, or remain hiding in water, or sneak into an iron cage and remain therein, or go and conceal himself in the infernal regions – even then death would not let him escape. Moreover, whatever, one may be – whether learned or a fool, rich or poor, wise or unwise, strong or weak – still, this all-devouring death lets no one escape.

"The full duration of a man's life is a hundred years; of this, half passes away in night, and half of the half in childhood and old age; the remainder is spent in contention, the separation from those we love, and affliction. Further, the soul that is, is as restless as a watery wave; how, then, can it yield man any peace?

"And now, in this Iron Age, to meet with truthful men is a difficult matter; while countries are daily laid waste, kings are avaricious, the earth yields little fruit, thieves and evil doers commit violence on the earth, and but little of religion, devotion and truth remain in the world; kings are tyrannical, Brahmans covetous, men have fallen under the influence of women, wives have become wanton, sons have begun reviling their fathers, and friends have begun to display enmity. Observe, further, that death did not even spare the great Abhimanyu, whose maternal uncle was Kanhaiya, and father Arjun. And when Yama carries off a man, wealth remains behind in his house, and father, mother, wife, son, brothers and kindred – no one proves of any avail; his good and evil deeds, his vices and his virtues alone accompany him; while those same kinsfolk take him to the burning-ground and burn him.

"And see how the night comes to an end on one side, while day dawns on the other; here the moon sets, there the sun rises. In the same way youth departs, old age comes on; thus, also, time goes on passing and yet, even while perceiving this, man does not learn wisdom.

"Observe, again, in the First, or Golden Age, Mandhata, a great king, who filled the whole earth with the fame of his virtue; and in the second, or Silver Age, the glorious monarch Ramachandra, who, bridging the sea, destroyed such a fortress as Lanka, and slew Ravana; and in the Third Age, Yudhisthira reigned in such a manner that people sing of his renown to this day–yet death did not spare even these.

"Moreover, the birds which fly in the air, and the animals which dwell in the sea, when the hour arrives, even these fall into trouble. No one has escaped sorrow on coming into this world. To grieve on this account is folly. It is best, therefore, to practise religious duties."

When Vishnusharma had reasoned with him in this manner, it came into the Brahman's mind that he would thenceforth perform meritorious and pious acts. Having thought this over in his mind, he said to his sons, "I am about to sit down to a sacrifice; you go and bring me a turtle from the sea."

On receiving their father's command, they went to a fisherman and said, "Take a rupee, and catch a turtle for us."

He took it, and caught one, and gave it to them.

Then the eldest of the brothers said to the second, "Do thou take it up?"

He replied, "I will not touch it; a bad smell will cling to my hands, and I am very fastidious in the matter of eating."

The second said, "I am very particular in my social contacts with women."

The eldest said, "I am particular about enjoying sound sleep."

Thus did the three of them begin wrangling; and leaving the turtle where it was, they proceeded, seeking justice, to the king and said to the gatekeeper, "Three Brahmans have come seeking justice; go and tell this to the king."

On hearing this, the doorkeeper went and informed the king.

The king summoned them, and asked, "Why are you quarrelling one with another?"

Then the youngest of them said, "Your majesty! I am very particular about my food."

The second said, "Lord of the earth! I want to be presentable before women."

The eldest said, " Incarnation of justice! I am particular in the matter of beds."

When the monarch heard these he said, "Each of you submit to a trial."

They replied, "Very well."

The king sent for his cook, and ordered,

"prepare various kinds of condiments and meats, and give this Brahman a thoroughly good repast."

On hearing this, the cook went and prepared food and taking with him the one who was nice in the matter of food, seated him in front of the dishes. He was on the point of taking up a mouthful and putting it into his mouth, when an offensive smell came from it. He let it go, washed his hands, and came to the king.

The king asked, "Didst thou enjoy thy repast?"

The he replied, "Your majesty! I perceived a disagreeable smell in the food, and did not eat."

The king asked again, "State the cause of the offensive smell."

He replied, "Your majesty! It was rice which had been grown on a burning-ground; the smell of corpses proceeded from it, and hence I did not eat it."

On hearing this, the king summoned his steward and asked, "Sirrah! From what village does this rice come?"

He replied, "From Shibpur, your majesty!" The king gave the command, "Summon the landholder of that village."

Thereupon the steward had the landholder brought before the monarch. The king asked him, "On what land was this rice grown?"

He replied, "On a burning-ground, your majesty!"

When the king heard this, he said to that

Brahman, "Thou art indeed a connoisseur in the matter of food."

After this, he had the one who was nice in the matter of women sent for and with a bed laid out in an apartment, and all the requisites for enjoyment placed therein, had a beautiful woman brought and placed near him, and the two while lying down began conversing with each other.

The king was secretly looking on through a lattice.

Now, the Brahman was about to give her a kiss, when smelling her breath, he turned his face away, and went to sleep.

The king having witnessed this conduct, entered his palace and sought repose.

Rising early in the morning, he came into the court and summoned that Brahman, and asked, "O Brahman! Didst thou pass the night pleasantly?"

He replied, "Your majesty! I found no pleasure."

"Why?" asked the king again.

The Brahman replied, "The smell of a goat proceeded from her mouth and my mind was much distressed in consequence."

When the king heard this, he summoned the attendant and inquired, "Whence didst thou bring this woman? and who is she?"

She said, "She is my sister's daughter; her mother died when she was three months old, and I brought her up on goat's milk."

On hearing this, the monarch said, "Thou art indeed a connoisseur in respect of women."

After that, the king had a very fine bed prepared, and caused the Brahman who was a nice judge of beds to sleep thereon.

As it was morning, the king sent for him, and asked, "Didst thou sleep comfortably through the night?"

He replied, "your majesty! I had no sleep the whole night long."

"Why?" asked the king.

He replied, "Your majesty! In the seventh fold of the bedding there was a hair, which was pricking my back, and I had no sleep in consequence."

On hearing this, the king looked into the seventh fold of the bedding, and lo! A hair was found. Thereupon he said to him, "Thou art indeed a nice judge of beds."

After relating so much of the story, the ghoul asked, "Who was the greatest connoisseur of those three?"

King Vikramaditya replied, "He who was the connoisseur of beds."

When the ghoul heard this, he went again and hung on that tree; and the king also went there on the instant, and bound him, placed him on his shoulder and carried him away.

❐ ❐ ❐

24. YAGYA SHARMA'S SON

The ghoul said:

"Your majesty! In the country of Kalinga there was a Brahman named Yagya Sharma, whose wife was Somadatta. She was very beautiful.

The Brahman began offering sacrifices, whereupon his wife gave birth to a beautiful boy. When he attained the age of five years, his father began teaching him the Shastras. At the age of twelve years he had finished the study of all the Shatras, and became a great scholar; and he began to be in constant attendance upon his father to help him.

After the lapse of some time the boy died, and in their sorrow for him his parents uttered loud cries of lamentation and wailing.

On receiving this news all his kinsfolk hastened thither, and fastening the boy upon a bier, took him away to the burning-ground; and when there, began repeatedly gazing at him, and said to one another, "See! Even in death he appears beautiful!"

They were uttering words like these, and arranging the pyre, while an ascetic was also seated there engaged in religious austerity. He, hearing these words began to think to himself, "My body has become very old; if I enter this boy's body, I can practise religious meditation with ease and comfort."

Having thought thus, he entered the body of the child, turned round, and pronouncing the names of Ram (Balaram) and Kirshna, sat up as one sits up from sleep.

When the people witnessed this, they all returned to their homes in astonishment; his father lost all desire for the world on witnessing this marvel; first he laughed, then he wept.

After relating so much of the story, the ghoul asked, "Say, your majesty, why he laughed, and why he wept?"

Thereupon the king replied, "Seeing the ascetic enter his body, and so learning the art of changing one's own body for another he laughed; and through regret at having to quit his own body he wept, thinking, "Thus shall I too some day have to abandon my own body."

Hearing this, the ghoul went again and suspended himself on that tree; and the king, too, arriving close at his heels, bound him, put him on his shoulder, and carried him away.

❐ ❐ ❐

25. V-DAY FOR VIKRAMADITYA

Then the ghoul said:

Your majesty! There was a city in the south named Dharmpur, the king of which was named Mahabal.

Once upon a time another king of that same region led an army against and invaded his capital. He continued fighting for several days. When his army went over in part to the enemy, and a portion was cut to pieces, then, having no help for it, he took his wife and daughter with him and went forth by night into the jungle.

After he had penetrated several miles into the jungle, the day broke and a village came in view. Then, leaving the queen and princess seated beneath a tree, he went himself towards the village to get something to eat and in the meantime a body of Bhils came and surrounded him and asked him to throw down his arms.

On hearing this, the king commenced discharging arrows, and they did the same from their side. Thus did the fight last for three hours, and several of the Bhils were slain. In the meantime, an arrow struck the king's forehead with such force that he reeled and fell, and one of them came up and cut off the king's head.

When the queen and princess saw the king dead, they took their way back to the jungle weeping and beating their breasts. After having proceeded a mile or two thus, they got tired and sat down, and began to be troubled by many an anxious thought.

During this time a king, named Chandrasena, together with his son, while pursuing the game, came into that jungle and the king noticing the footprints of the two women, said to his son, "How could the footprints of human feet appear in this vast forest?"

The prince replied, "your majesty ! These are women's foot-prints – a man's foot is not so small."

The king observed, "True, man has not got such delicate feet."

The prince said again, "They have just this moment passed."

The monarch said, "Come, let us seek them in the jungle; if we find them, I will give her whose foot is large to thee; and I will take the other."

Having entered into this mutual contract, they went forward, and perceived the two seated.

They were delighted on seeing them and seating them on their horses in the manner agreed upon, they brought them home. The prince took possession of the queen and the king of the princess.

Having related so much of the story, the ghoul asked, "Your majesty! What relationship will there be between the children of these two?"

On hearing this, the king held his tongue through ignorance.

Then the ghoul said in great glee, "Your majesty! I have been highly pleased at witnessing your patience and courage; I tell you one thing, however; do you attend thereto – one, the hairs of whose body are like thorns, and whose body itself is like wood, and whose name is Shantshil, has come into your city and he it is who has deputed you to fetch me, while he himself is seated in the burning-ground working his spells, and desires to kill you.

"I therefore forewarn you, that when he has finished his devotions, he will say to you, 'Your majesty! Prostrate yourself so that eight parts of your body may touch the ground.' You should then say, 'I am the king of kings, and all potentates bow low in salutation before me; up to this hour I have not bowed in adoration to any one, and I know not how to do so, you are a spiritual teacher, kindly show me how to do so, and then will I do it.' When he bows down, give him such a blow with your sword that his head may become severed from his body; then will you reign uninterruptedly; whereas, if you will not do this, he will slay you, and reign permanently."

Having warned the king in these words, the ghoul came out of that corpse, and went his way; and while somewhat of night still remained, the king brought the corpse and placed it before the ascetic.

The ascetic became glad on seeing it and lauded the king greatly. After that, he repeated incantations and raised the corpse to life and gave a burnt-offering in sacrifice: and sitting with his face southwards, offered to his god all the materials he had prepared; and after offering up betel leaf, flowers, incense, lamps, and consecrated food, he said to the king, "Make obeisance; very glorious will thy dignity become and the eight supernatural faculties will always abide in thy house."

On hearing this, the king called to mind the words of the ghoul, and joining his hands, said with the utmost humility, "Your reverence! I know not how to bow in adoration; you, however, are a spiritual teacher; if you will kindly teach me, I will do it."

As the ascetic, on hearing this, lowered his head to prostrate himself, that instant the king struck him such a blow with his sword that his head was severed; and the ghoul came and showered down flowers. It is declared that there is nothing unlawful in slaying him who would himself slay another.

At that time Indra and the rest of the gods, having witnessed the king's courage, mounted their cars and cheered the king. And Indra said in pleasure to King Vikramaditya, "Ask a boon."

Then the king joined his hands and said, "Your majesty! Let this story concerning me become famous in the world."

Indra replied, "So long as the moon, sun, earth and sky endure, this story shall be famous; and thou shalt be ruler over the whole earth."

After saying this, king Indra went to his place, and King Vikramaditya took those two corpses and threw them both into the oil-cauldron.

Thereupon the two heroes came and presented themselves and began to say, "What command is there for us?"

The king replied, "When I remember you, then do you come."

Taking from them their promise to do this, the king returned home and began to attend to his government. It is said that whether one be learned or a fool, a child or a man, he alone who is wise will win success.

❒ ❒ ❒